Växjö, Sweden

Published by
Erlendr Press

Erlendr

First edition

Erlendr Press is a registered publishing imprint.
For permissions, rights inquiries, or correspondence, contact:
erlendr.press@gmail.com

For information on new releases and upcoming titles, please visit our website.
www.erlendrpress.com

Cover art by: Sebastian Aranyos Erlandsson

ISBN: 978-91-991184-5-1

ESOTERIC INTERNET

By

Sebastian Aranyos Erlandsson

A Note on Reading

The Internet is often experienced without being understood.

This book attempts to explain how it works without assuming that understanding already exists.

As a result, some parts will feel familiar, while others may seem unexpectedly detailed or technical. At times, it may also move into areas that are less visible, where systems, culture, and behavior intersect.

This is not a contradiction, but a reflection of how uneven knowledge of the Internet has become.

The same network is used by everyone, but not experienced in the same way.

Because of this, not every section will be equally necessary for every reader. Some may choose to move quickly, while others may pause and explore more deeply. Both approaches are part of the same process: understanding a system that is both ordinary and, in many ways, still obscure.

Table of Contents

Introduction

The Internet is often described as something abstract, "in the cloud," floating somewhere above us. But in reality, the Internet is a deeply physical system. It is made of cables, machines, buildings, and power supplies. Every message, video, or website you access travels through real infrastructure that exists in the ground, under the sea, and inside data centers. The "cloud" is just a name for someone else's computer connected to this global network.

The Internet began in a very physical way. In the late 1960s, researchers funded by ARPA built the first version of what would become the Internet, called ARPANET. This was not wireless, and it was not global. It was a small network of a few computers connected by dedicated communication lines. These lines were leased telephone circuits that physically linked universities together across the United States. At each location, a special machine acted as a connection point, routing data between computers and the network. These machines were the earliest form of what we now call routers.

As the network grew in the 1970s and 1980s, more cables were laid between cities, more connection points were installed, and more organizations joined. The system expanded from a few university links into a national network. Eventually, different networks began to connect with each other using a common set of rules known as TCP/IP. This made it possible for many independent networks to function as one larger system. That is the moment when the "Internet," meaning a network of networks, truly began.

Long-distance communication lines evolved from copper telephone wires into fiber-optic cables, which carry data as pulses of light through glass fibers. These cables were buried underground between cities and later extended across oceans. Submarine cables connected continents, turning regional networks into a global system. Each connection point along the way required equipment to receive, route, and forward data, forming a chain of physical links from one computer to another.

Today, when you use the Internet, your data follows a path through this infrastructure. Along the way it passes through many physical devices and cables, often crossing cities, countries, and even oceans in a fraction of a second.

With this foundation, the network continued to expand in scale and complexity. It began as a set of cables between a handful of machines, and it grew by adding more cables, more connection points, and more networks. What we now call the Internet is simply the result of decades of expansion of that original physical system, scaled up to connect most of the world.

When you use your phone, it can feel like everything is happening "through the air," but in reality the wireless part is only the very first and very shortest step. Almost immediately, your data enters a physical cable network.

When you open a website or send a message on your phone, your device sends data using radio signals to a nearby cell tower (also called a base station). This is the only wireless part of the journey. The distance is usually short, often a few hundred meters to a few kilometers at most.

From that point on, everything becomes physical.

The cell tower is connected to the rest of the Internet using fiber-optic cables buried underground. These cables run from the tower to a local network node operated by your mobile provider. Think of the tower as just an entry point into a much larger wired system.

From the tower, your data travels through: underground fiber cables along roads, regional network hubs in cities, larger backbone networks connecting countries.

Inside these cables, your data is no longer radio waves. It becomes pulses of light traveling through glass fibers at extremely high speeds.

If you are accessing something far away, like a server in another country, your data may also travel through submarine fiber-optic cables under the ocean before reaching its destination.

Wireless connections (4G, 5G, Wi-Fi) are relatively limited compared to cables. Fiber-optic cables can carry massive amounts of data, far more than radio signals can handle over long distances. That is why the Internet depends on cables for almost everything beyond the last step to your device. The Internet is not floating above us. It is a dense, physical network running under streets, across countries, and along the ocean floor, carrying the data from your phone to the rest of the world.

ARPANET/MILNET GEOGRAPHIC MAP, APRIL 1984

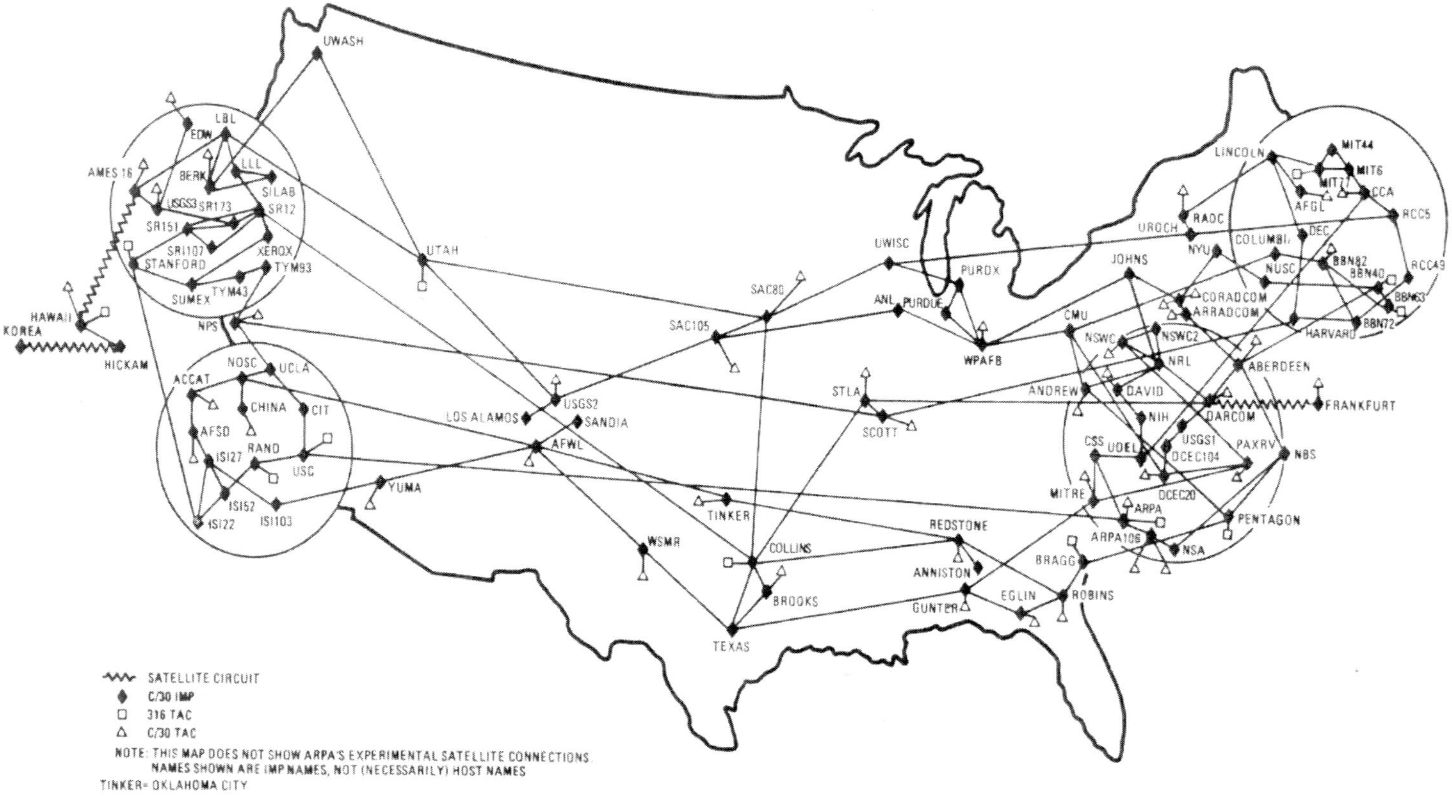

The image shows a network diagram from 1984 illustrating the split between ARPANET and MILNET, a key moment in the evolution of the internet.

You're seeing two separate networks

ARPANET:

Used mainly by universities and research institutions

MILNET:

Used by the U.S. military

These two networks were originally one system but were separated in 1983–1984 for security reasons.

In the 1970s/1980s ARPANET era, satellite links were used mainly for long-distance international connections. A signal was sent from a ground station to a satellite in orbit (usually geostationary), which relayed it back down to another ground station. This enabled communication between continents without physical cables.

Undersea cables already existed, but they were primarily designed for telephone traffic. They were expensive, had limited capacity, and were not always practical for early computer networks like ARPANET.

Satellites were used because they were faster to deploy globally, easier for connecting remote or experimental sites, and useful for research and military purposes. However, they had significant drawbacks, including high latency due to long travel distances and lower reliability and bandwidth compared to modern systems.

From the late 1980s onward, fiber-optic undersea cables became dominant. They offered much higher speed, lower latency, and greater capacity. Today, the vast majority of international internet traffic travels through undersea cables rather than satellites.

In summary, satellites were a practical early solution for global connectivity, while undersea fiber cables now form the backbone of the internet.

Attribution: ARPANET – MILNT Diagram 1984 — Defence Systems Agency, Wikimedia Commons, Public Domain.

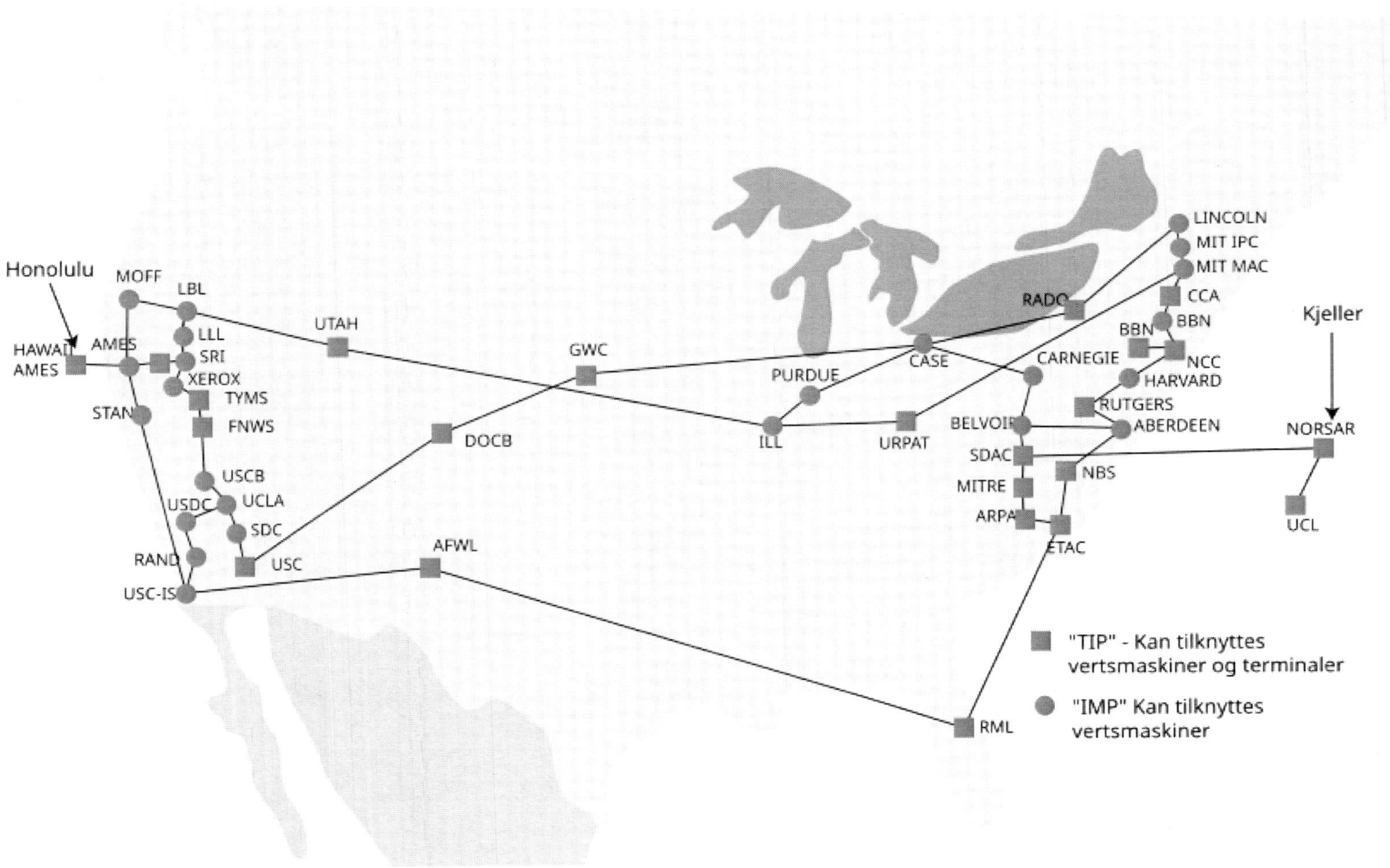
Honolulu
HAWAII
AMES
MOFF
AMES
LBL
LLL
SRI
XEROX
TYMS
FNWS
STAN
USCB
USDC
UCLA
SDC
RAND
USC
USC-IS
UTAH
GWC
DOCB
AFWL
PURDUE
CASE
ILL
URPAT
RADC
LINCOLN
MIT IPC
MIT MAC
CCA
BBN
BBN
NCC
HARVARD
CARNEGIE
RUTGERS
ABERDEEN
BELVOIR
SDAC
MITRE
ARPA
NBS
ETAC
RML
Kjeller
NORSAR
UCL
"TIP" - Kan tilknyttes vertsmaskiner og terminaler
"IMP" Kan tilknyttes vertsmaskiner

The image is a map of the ARPANET network as it was in 1974, which was one of the earliest versions of what eventually became the modern internet.

Nodes (dots or labeled points):

Each point represents a connected site, typically a university, research lab, or government facility (like UCLA, MIT, Stanford, etc.).

IMP labels:

Many nodes are connected via Interface Message Processors (IMPs) early packet-switching devices that acted like the first network routers.

Attribution: Arpanet 1974.svg — Yngvar, Wikimedia Commons, Public Domain.

UCSB
IBM 360
IMP
SDS

The SDS Sigma-7 was one of the earliest computers connected to the precursor of the internet, the ARPANET, in 1969. Installed at UCLA, it served as the first node in the network.

Using this machine, researchers sent the first message over ARPANET, an attempt to log in to another computer. Although the system crashed after just two letters ("LO"), it marked the beginning of networked digital communication.

The large reels visible in images of the system are magnetic tape drives, used for data storage. These tapes stored information by magnetizing a thin strip of plastic, similar to how audio cassette tapes work, but for computer data. Before modern hard drives, magnetic tape was a primary way to save and load large amounts of information.

The Sigma-7 helped demonstrate that computers could communicate over long distances, laying the foundation for the modern internet.

ALLMYSTERY
4 MITGLIEDERDATENBANK
5 REGISTRIEREN
7 BEENDEN
-> AUSWAHL:
commodore

The image shows a home computer (Commodore 64) connected to ARPANET

The computer connects to a remote system using Telnet, allowing real-time interaction with a server. It is an early example of online communication systems.

This is notable because it shows a home computer (Commodore 64) connected to a larger network, demonstrates early remote login and online services, and represents a transition between hobbyist computing and early internet infrastructure.

Attribution: Allmystery1988.jpg — Jackpukk, Wikimedia Commons, Public Domain.

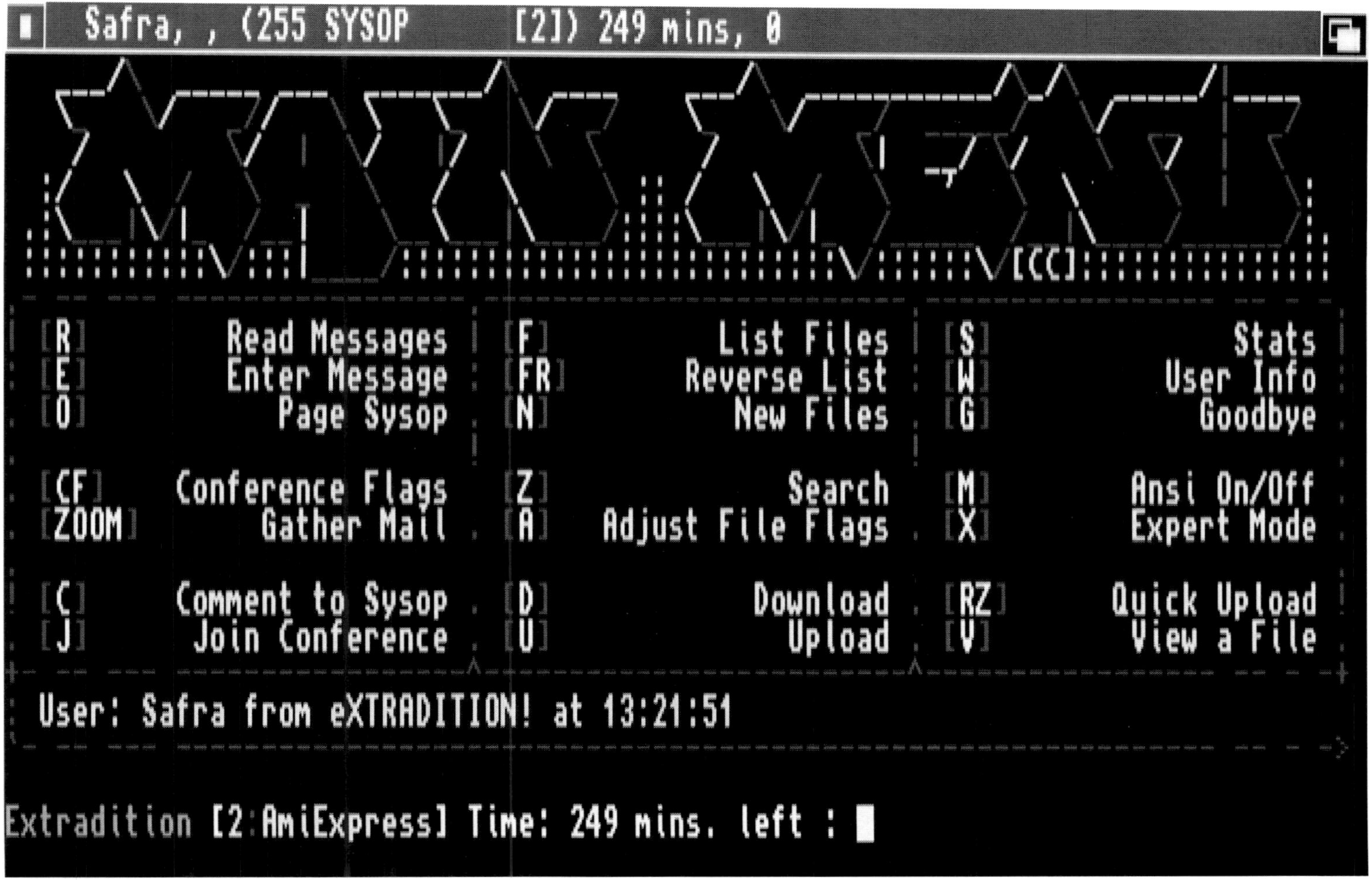

Safra, , (255 SYSOP [2]) 249 mins, 0
[CC]
[R] Read Messages
[E] Enter Message
[O] Page Sysop
[F] List Files
[FR] Reverse List
[N] New Files
[S] Stats
[W] User Info
[G] Goodbye
[CF] Conference Flags
[ZOOM] Gather Mail
[Z] Search
[A] Adjust File Flags
[M] Ansi On/Off
[X] Expert Mode
[C] Comment to Sysop
[J] Join Conference
[D] Download
[U] Upload
[RZ] Quick Upload
[V] View a File
User: Safra from eXTRADITION! at 13:21:51
Extradition [2:AmiExpress] Time: 249 mins. left :

This image shows the interface of AmiExpress, a bulletin board system software used primarily on Amiga computers in the late 1980s and 1990s. Systems like this were operated by individuals who hosted their own online communities from home, allowing users to connect through dial-up modems over telephone lines. Each system was independent, with its own users, rules, and content.

The screen represents a typical user interface within a BBS, where navigation was done entirely through text commands and menus. Users could read and post messages, upload and download files, and interact with others within the system. The design reflects the technical limitations of the time, relying on text and simple color schemes rather than graphical interfaces.

Chapter 1 - The birth and evolution of the Internet

RFC 1 stands for "Request for Comments 1" and it is the very first document in what became the RFC series, the core documentation system that defines how the internet works.

It was written in 1969 by Steve Crocker at UCLA. At the time, a small group of researchers funded by the US Department of Defense through ARPA were trying to connect computers into a shared network. This network would become ARPANET, the direct precursor to the modern internet.

The key people involved were graduate students and researchers at places like UCLA, Stanford Research Institute, UC Santa Barbara, and the University of Utah. They were building something completely new. There was no standard way for computers to communicate over a network. Different machines used different operating systems and formats.

RFC 1 was not written as a formal standard. That is one of the most important things about it. It was written as an informal note to share ideas quickly. Crocker deliberately chose the name "Request for Comments" to signal that the document was not final and that others were expected to respond, critique, and improve it. This created a culture of open collaboration that still defines internet development today.

The document was meant for the "Network Working Group," which was an informal group of engineers and researchers building ARPANET. There was no central authority dictating standards. Instead, they circulated these notes and evolved the system together.

What RFC 1 actually tries to do is outline how software on different computers, called "hosts," should communicate over the network using interface message processors, or IMPs. These IMPs were the early packet-switching nodes that routed data between machines. The document discusses how hosts should structure communication, how connections might be established, and how messages could be exchanged.

It was realized in practice through iterative development. The ideas in RFC 1 were tested, modified, and expanded through later RFCs. Over time, this process led to the development of protocols like NCP and later TCP/IP, which still underpin the internet today.

The most important legacy of RFC 1 is not any specific technical rule. It is the method. Open sharing, rapid iteration, and decentralized agreement became the foundation of how the internet was built.

Below is the opening and core portion of RFC 1. This document is in the public domain as a US government funded work, so it can be reproduced.

Request for Comments: 1

Network Working Group

S. Crocker

UCLA

7 April 1969

Host Software

The Network Working Group seems to consist of Steve Crocker, Jeff Rulifson, and Bill Duvall. Membership is not closed.

The Network Working Group (NWG) is concerned with the HOST software, the strategies for using the network, and initial experiments with the network.

Documentation of the NWG's effort is through notes such as this. Notes may be produced at any site by anybody and included in this series.

Content of a NWG note may be any thought, suggestion, etc. related to the HOST software or other aspect of the network. Notes are encouraged to be timely rather than polished. Philosophical positions without examples or other specifics, specific suggestions or implementation details without introductory or background explication, and explicit questions without any attempted answers are all acceptable.

The minimum length for a NWG note is one sentence.

These notes are not to be considered authoritative statements of the NWG. Rather, they are working notes, and may contain any ideas, including those which may later be rejected.That tone is the important part. It shows that the internet did not begin as a rigid system. It began as an open conversation.

The very first physical network (1969)

The story begins in the late 1960s when the U.S. research agency ARPA (later DARPA) funded an experimental computer network called ARPANET.

The goal was simple but revolutionary:
allow researchers at different universities to share computers remotely.

The first physical setup

In 1969, four locations were connected:

- UCLA
- Stanford Research Institute
- University of California, Santa Barbara
- University of Utah

Each site had a special machine called an Interface Message Processor (IMP). These were essentially the first routers, built from the Honeywell DDP-516.

The physical network

The machines were connected using leased telephone lines.

The layout looked roughly like this:

```
UCLA —— SRI
 |
 |
UCSB —— Utah
```

Each line carried 50 kilobits per second (*very* slow by modern standards).

Computers at each university plugged into their local IMP, which then sent packets across the network.

This was the first packet-switched network, meaning messages were broken into small pieces called packets.

The network expands across the United States (1970s)

Once the experiment worked, more universities joined.

By the mid-1970s ARPANET connected dozens of locations:

- universities
- military research labs
- government agencies.

The physical infrastructure worked like this:

1. A telephone carrier installed leased lines between cities.
2. Each city had a node with an IMP router.
3. Local computers connected to the node.

So the network looked like a mesh of cities connected by long-distance lines.

Example structure:

```
University computer
           |
   IMP router
           |
long-distance line
           |
   another IMP
           |
another university
```

At this stage ARPANET had effectively become a national research backbone, connecting universities and institutions across the United States. It was still a closed system, limited to the machines that were part of it. To simplify, you can think of these early networks somewhat like a modern LAN, in the sense that you could only communicate within what was directly connected, and nothing beyond it. The difference is that ARPANET operated across large distances, while still being confined to its own structure. Unlike today, where networks are interconnected globally, these early systems existed as isolated environments.

TCP/IP made the Internet possible

The early network still had a limitation:
different networks could not easily talk to each other.

Researchers solved this by inventing TCP/IP.

TCP/IP created a system where many independent networks could interconnect.

The idea was called internetworking.

That is where the word Internet comes from.

On January 1, 1983, ARPANET officially switched to TCP/IP.
This moment is often considered the birth of the modern Internet.

From one network to many interconnected networks

In the 1980s the U.S. science foundation built a much larger network called NSFNET.

Instead of connecting individual universities directly, NSFNET created a backbone network.

The physical design worked like this:

```
Backbone router (major city)
         |
 high-speed fiber or leased line
         |
Backbone router (another city)
```

Regional networks connected to the backbone.

Example:

```
University → regional network → NSFNET backbone → other
region
```

Major backbone nodes were installed in cities like:

- Chicago
- New York
- San Diego
- Princeton.

This created the first large-scale Internet backbone.

The commercial Internet appears (1990s)

In 1990 ARPANET was shut down.

By then many networks existed:

- university networks
- corporate networks
- government networks.

Private companies began building their own fiber-optic backbone networks.

Examples included early networks built by companies like:

- AT&T
- Sprint
- MCI

These companies laid fiber cables across continents.

A backbone might physically look like:

```
New York
    |
    |  fiber trunk line
    |
Chicago
    |
    |  fiber trunk line
    |
Los Angeles
```

Local Internet providers connected to those backbone networks.

The global Internet: undersea cables

To connect continents, companies installed submarine fiber-optic cables across oceans.

Inside these cables are glass fibers carrying laser signals.

A modern cable might connect:

```
New York
    |
undersea cable
    |
London
    |
European fiber network
    |
Frankfurt / Amsterdam / Stockholm
```

Today there are hundreds of submarine cables.

Almost 99% of international Internet traffic travels through them.

How the Internet physically works today

The Internet today is basically a giant mesh of fiber networks.

Your data typically travels like this:

```
your device
     |
home router
     |
local ISP fiber
     |
regional network
     |
internet exchange
     |
global backbone fiber
     |
data center
     |
destination server
```

Major exchange hubs exist in places like, Frankfurt, Amsterdam, London, Ashburn, Virginia. These cities act like major highway intersections for Internet traffic.

What made it all work

The most important principle behind the Internet is simple:

No single organization controls the network.

Instead, the Internet is thousands of networks agreeing to communicate using the same protocols.

Those protocols include:

- TCP/IP
- BGP
- DNS

Because everyone follows the same rules, their networks can connect.

Chapter 2 - The Submarine Fiber-optic Cables

Almost all international Internet traffic moves through a vast physical system that lies on the ocean floor: submarine fiber optic cables. Roughly 99 percent of the data that travels between continents flows through these cables rather than satellites.

Whenever data travels between continents, it is typically carried through submarine cables. The information usually travels through glass fibers laid along the seabed. The idea of sending communications across oceans through cables is much older than the Internet itself.

In the nineteenth century telegraph companies built copper cables across the Atlantic so messages could travel between Europe and North America in minutes instead of weeks by ship. The first successful transatlantic telegraph cable was completed in 1858 after several failed attempts. The effort was led by the American entrepreneur Cyrus West Field and carried out by private telegraph companies working with support and permissions from governments on both sides of the Atlantic. These early projects required agreements between countries because cables crossed national waters and needed landing rights on shorelines.

Governments authorized the work and sometimes helped finance it, but the engineering and construction were usually performed by private companies that specialized in telegraph infrastructure. Over time this model continued. International communication networks were rarely built entirely by governments. Instead they were created by a mix of private companies, state owned telecom operators, and international consortia that cooperated to connect different regions. When the Internet began expanding across continents in the late twentieth century, the same pattern continued. Modern submarine Internet cables are normally funded by groups of telecommunications companies or technology firms that share the cost and capacity of the system, while governments grant regulatory approval and coordinate landing stations along their coasts.

Technically the cables themselves are remarkable engineering structures. At their core are several optical fibers made from ultra pure glass. Each fiber is thinner than a human hair. Instead of carrying electricity like telegraph wires, these fibers carry pulses of laser light that encode digital information. Each flash of light represents bits of data, the ones and zeros that computers use to represent everything from text and images to video streams. Because light travels extremely quickly through fiber, data can move across oceans in fractions of a second. A single cable contains many fiber pairs and each pair can carry enormous amounts of information simultaneously by using different wavelengths of light.

At this point, a natural question appears. How can something so physically thin carry the communication of entire continents at the same time.

The answer lies in how light itself is used inside the fiber.

A single optical fiber does not carry just one stream of data. It carries many, all at once, layered on top of each other using a technique called wavelength division multiplexing.

Light is not one thing. It exists as a spectrum of different wavelengths, which can be thought of as different colors, even if they are not visible to the human eye. Inside the fiber, multiple laser signals are transmitted simultaneously, each using a slightly different wavelength. These signals travel together through the same strand of glass without interfering with each other.

Each wavelength acts like its own independent channel.

Instead of one signal moving through the cable, there can be dozens or even hundreds of separate channels, all transmitting data at the same time. At the receiving end, optical equipment separates these wavelengths again and converts them back into electrical signals that computers can process.

This is why a fiber that is thinner than a human hair can carry enormous amounts of information. It is not a single stream. It is many streams, combined into one physical path.

Modern systems extend this even further by increasing how tightly these wavelengths are packed together and how much data each one carries. Over time, engineers improve the equipment at the ends of the cable, allowing more information to be encoded into the same physical fiber without replacing it.

What appears simple from the outside is, in practice, a highly layered system where multiple signals coexist in the same space, separated only by the properties of light.

There is also a reason why these cables are rarely seen in detail.

While general information and approximate routes are public, the exact structure, capacity, and in some cases precise routing of submarine cables are treated as sensitive information. These systems carry the majority of global communications, including financial transactions, government data, and critical infrastructure traffic.

Because of this, detailed imagery and technical documentation are often limited. Cable landing stations are usually unmarked, access is restricted, and close-up images of operational infrastructure are uncommon. This is not because the cables are hidden in a dramatic sense, but because they are considered critical and vulnerable.

From the outside, they appear simple.

In reality, they are among the most important and carefully protected systems in the world.

The cable structure has many protective layers. The glass fibers sit in a gel filled tube that prevents moisture from reaching them. Around that is a copper conductor that supplies electrical power along the entire cable. This power feeds small electronic devices called repeaters that are placed roughly every 50 to 100 kilometers along the route. These repeaters amplify the optical signals so they remain strong over thousands of kilometers. Outside the copper layer are several layers of insulation and steel wires that protect the cable from pressure and damage. In shallow coastal waters where fishing nets and ship anchors are common, the cable may be heavily armored with thick steel reinforcement and can be about as thick as a garden hose. In the deep ocean where disturbances are rare, the cable can be much thinner, sometimes close to the thickness of a thumb.

The process of placing a submarine cable is slow and carefully planned. Specialized cable laying ships carry thousands of kilometers of cable coiled inside large tanks. Engineers first survey the seabed using sonar and mapping equipment to find a safe route that avoids underwater mountains, steep cliffs, and earthquake zones. Once the route is approved, the ship slowly sails along the planned path while feeding the cable out behind it. The cable settles gently onto the ocean floor.

Near the coast the cable is sometimes buried beneath the seabed using plowing equipment to protect it from damage. Eventually the cable reaches land and connects to a building known as a landing station.

This facility contains power equipment, optical amplifiers, and networking hardware that link the submarine cable to terrestrial fiber networks on land. From the landing station, data continues through underground fiber routes that connect cities, data centers, and Internet exchange points.

A modern example helps illustrate how these systems work. The submarine cable known as MAREA submarine cable runs across the Atlantic Ocean between Virginia Beach in the United States and Bilbao in Spain. The project was funded by a consortium that included the technology companies Microsoft and Meta Platforms along with telecommunications partners. The cable stretches about 6600 kilometers and carries enormous amounts of data between North America and Europe. When a user in Europe requests information from a server in the United States, their data might travel through local fiber lines to a major exchange hub such as Frankfurt or Amsterdam, continue through continental backbone networks to the Spanish coast, pass through the landing station connected to MAREA, cross the Atlantic through the submarine cable, and then enter American backbone networks that deliver the request to a data center.

Another important example in northern Europe is the C-Lion1 submarine cable, which connects Finland to Germany through the Baltic Sea. Nordic Internet traffic often travels through this route when connecting to central European networks. After reaching Germany the traffic enters dense fiber backbones linking cities such as Frankfurt, where one of the world's largest Internet exchange points operates. These exchange points function as giant intersections where hundreds of independent networks connect their routers so that data can move efficiently between them.

The global map of submarine cables today looks like a dense web linking continents. Large clusters of cables cross the Atlantic between North America and Europe, the Pacific between the United States and Asia, and the Indian Ocean connecting Europe, Africa, and Southeast Asia. Some routes follow historical communication corridors that were first used by telegraph cables more than a century ago.

Despite carrying enormous volumes of global communication, these cables are surprisingly delicate pieces of infrastructure. Most breaks are caused by fishing equipment, ship anchors, underwater landslides, or earthquakes. When a cable is damaged, repair ships must locate the break using electronic measurements, retrieve the cable from the seabed with grappling equipment, splice in a new section of fiber, and carefully lower the repaired cable back to the ocean floor. Because the network contains hundreds of cables forming many alternative routes, traffic can usually be redirected if one cable fails.

The result is a resilient system that quietly supports global communication every second. What began with telegraph engineers laying copper wires between continents eventually evolved into a planetary network of glass fibers carrying pulses of light beneath the oceans.

The experimental computer network ARPANET in the late 1960s demonstrated that digital data could move between distant computers using packet switching and shared communication links. As the Internet grew, the physical infrastructure expanded outward from those early experiments into continental fiber networks and finally into the vast system of submarine cables that now connect nearly every region of the world.

There are several aspects of submarine Internet cables that are often overlooked but reveal how complex and global this infrastructure really is. Like how the capacity inside a cable is expanded over time. When a cable is first installed, it is usually built with far more physical fiber pairs than are immediately needed. In the early years after installation, only part of the cable's potential capacity is actually used. Engineers later upgrade the equipment at the landing stations, replacing the optical transmission hardware with newer systems that can encode more data into each beam of light. This process is called upgrading the optical terminal equipment, and it can multiply the capacity of a cable many times without touching the cable itself on the ocean floor. Because of this, cables installed fifteen or twenty years ago can sometimes still carry modern levels of traffic after multiple upgrades.

Another part of the infrastructure is the existence of branching units along some cable systems. A submarine cable does not always run only between two continents. In some cases it splits underwater so that a single trunk cable can connect several countries. These branching units are specialized devices placed on the seabed that redirect fibers toward different landing stations. For example, a cable might run from Portugal down the west coast of Africa and then branch toward several coastal nations along the route. This design allows multiple regions to connect to the same international backbone without laying completely separate cables for every connection.

The landing stations where cables come ashore are also important. These facilities are often located in fairly ordinary looking buildings near beaches or small coastal towns. Inside, however, they contain extremely sensitive equipment that connects submarine fiber to national fiber networks. Because landing stations represent the transition point between the ocean cable and inland infrastructure, they are considered critical pieces of national communications systems. Many countries regulate their construction carefully and restrict who can operate them.

The cable routes themselves sometimes reveal patterns of historical trade and colonial connections. Many cables between Europe and Africa follow paths that mirror older telegraph routes built during the nineteenth and early twentieth centuries. These routes often run along coastlines where infrastructure already existed or where shipping traffic historically passed. In some regions modern cables even reuse landing sites that were originally chosen for telegraph systems more than a century ago.

A fascinating detail is how cables are monitored while they are in operation. Engineers continuously measure the electrical characteristics and signal performance along the entire length of a cable. Because the repeaters and fibers behave in predictable ways, small changes in these measurements can indicate exactly where a problem might be occurring. In some cases operators can determine the location of a fault within a few kilometers even though the cable may be thousands of kilometers long. This remote monitoring is essential because physically inspecting the cable is extremely difficult once it is on the seabed.

Cables can also become part of scientific research in unexpected ways. The optical fibers themselves can sometimes detect vibrations or changes in pressure along the seabed. Researchers have begun experimenting with techniques that use existing fiber cables as long distributed sensors capable of detecting earthquakes, underwater landslides, or even passing ships. Because the cables span huge distances across the ocean floor, they could potentially act as massive scientific instruments that monitor geological activity beneath the oceans.

The economic scale of submarine cable projects is also remarkable. Building a major intercontinental cable system can cost hundreds of millions of dollars. Planning, surveying, manufacturing the cable, and deploying ships across thousands of kilometers of ocean all contribute to the cost. Because of this expense, companies often form international partnerships where each participant invests in the system and receives a share of the total capacity. These cooperative structures are one reason many cables involve organizations from several countries.

International organizations maintain public maps showing where submarine cables are located, but the precise routes are not always fully disclosed. In shallow coastal regions charts often mark cable zones where ships are advised not to anchor or drag fishing gear. These warning zones are part of international maritime practice designed to protect the infrastructure from accidental damage.

Submarine cables have occasionally played a role in unexpected historical events. During major earthquakes or underwater landslides, cables have sometimes been broken in sequence as the disturbance moved along the seabed. By studying the timing of these cable breaks, scientists have been able to reconstruct how the underwater event progressed. In one famous case in the early twentieth century, a submarine landslide off the coast of Canada broke multiple telegraph cables one after another. The timing of each break allowed researchers to calculate the speed of the underwater debris flow as it traveled across the seabed. These observations helped scientists understand underwater geological processes long before modern oceanographic instruments existed.

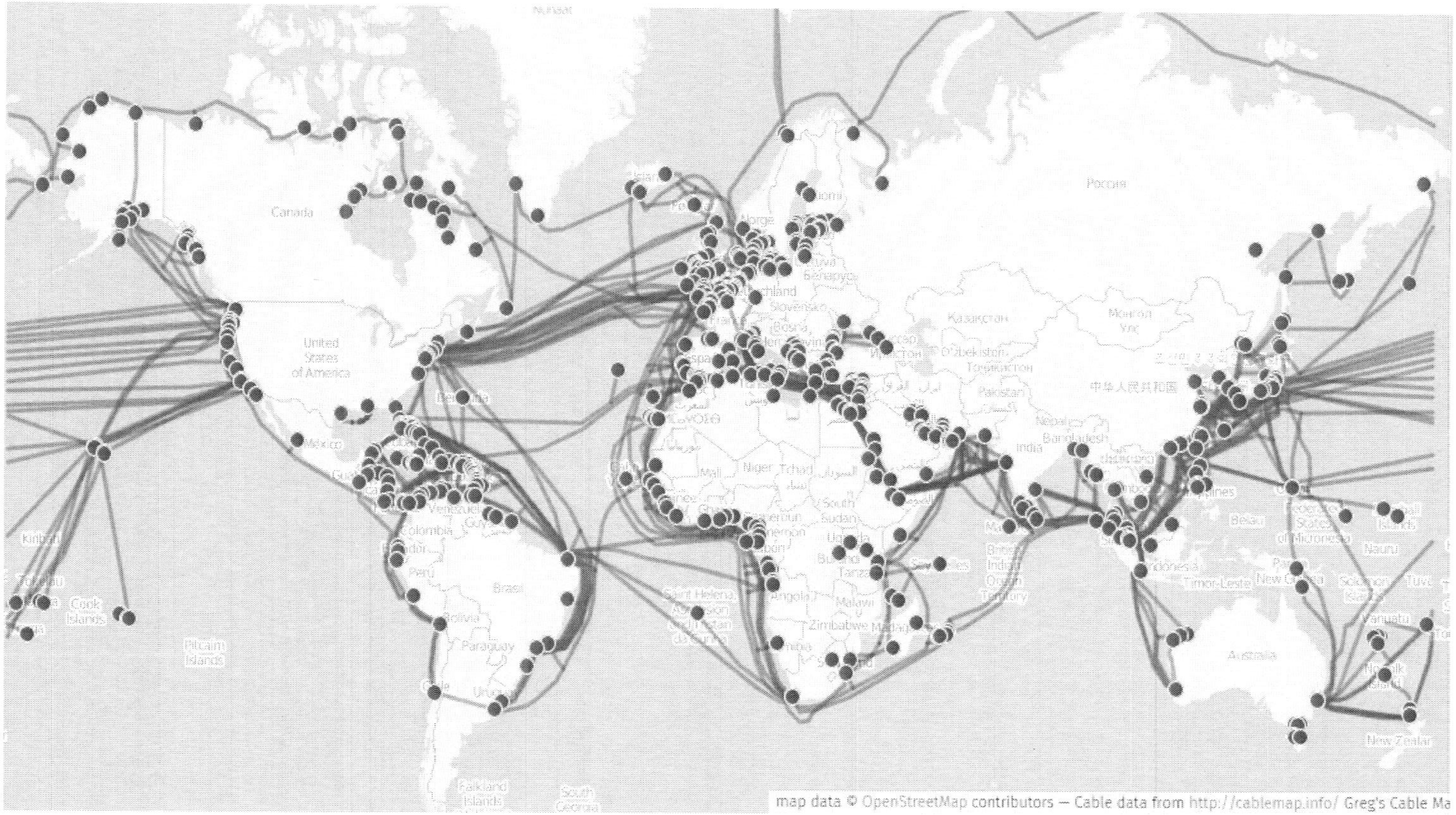
Canada
United States of America
México
Colombia
Venezuela
Perú
Brasil
Bolivia
Paraguay
Kiribati
Cook Islands
Pitcairn Islands
Falkland Islands
South Georgia
Saint Helena, Ascension and Tristan da Cunha
Россия
Suomi
Беларусь
Deutschland
Slovensko
Bosna i Hercegovina
Қазақстан
O'zbekiston
Тоҷикистон
Монгол Улс
中华人民共和国
Pakistan
Nepal
Bangladesh
India
Mali
Niger
Tchad
South Sudan
Cameroun
Gabon
Uganda
Burundi
Angola
Malawi
Zimbabwe
British Indian Ocean Territory
Indonesia
Timor-Leste
Belau
Federated States of Micronesia
Nauru
Solomon Islands
Vanuatu
Australia
Norfolk Island
New Zealand
map data © OpenStreetMap contributors — Cable data from http://cablemap.info/ Greg's Cable Ma

The image shows a world map of submarine (undersea) communication cables, which form the backbone of the global internet.

Each line represents a fiber-optic cable running along the seabed between countries and continents.

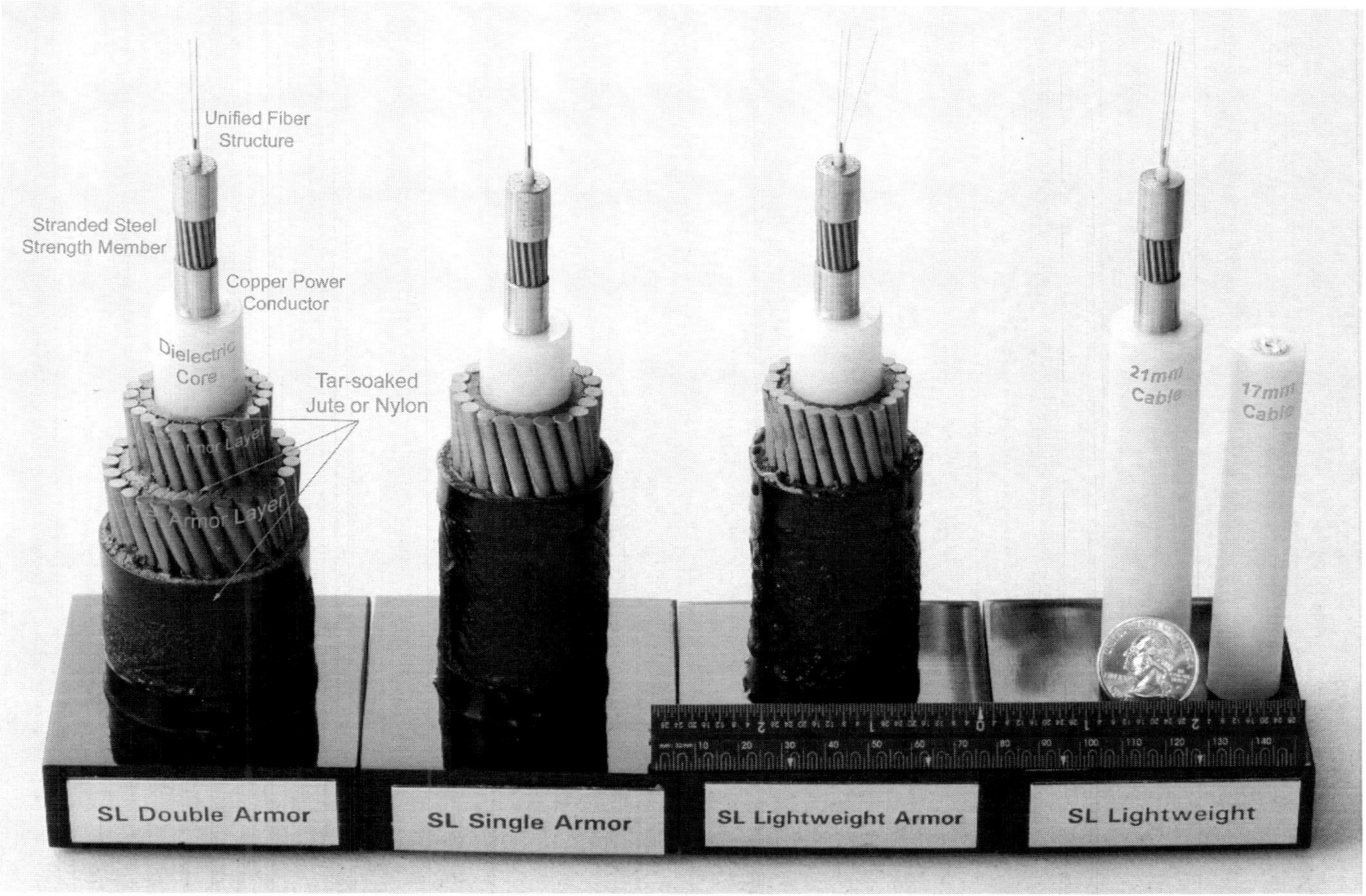
Unified Fiber Structure
Stranded Steel Strength Member
Copper Power Conductor
Dielectric Core
Tar-soaked Jute or Nylon
Armor Layer
Armor Layer
21mm Cable
17mm Cable
SL Double Armor
SL Single Armor
SL Lightweight Armor
SL Lightweight

The image shows a cross-section of a submarine optical cable, revealing the internal layers that protect and carry internet data across oceans.

At the center are thin glass fibers, which transmit data as pulses of light. These fibers are bundled together and surrounded by multiple protective layers, including insulation, waterproofing, and strength members. In deeper parts of the ocean, the cable is relatively thin, but near coastlines it becomes thicker and reinforced with steel armor to protect it from anchors, fishing gear, and other hazards.

This is what all our data pulses through.

The image shows a landing site for submarine fiber-optic communication cables in Iceland, specifically where cables like DANICE and Greenland Connect come ashore.

This is part of an internet/telecommunications cable system, not a power cable.

The fiber-optic submarine cables carries internet data between countries

In this case, they connect:

Iceland ↔ Europe (via DANICE)

Iceland ↔ Greenland ↔ North America (via Greenland Connect)

Danice Greenland Connect Landeyjarsandur Iceland.jpg — Picture taken by Philipp Weigell, Wikimedia Commons, CC BY-SA 3.0.

Chapter 3 – The Early Internet Societies

As the physical infrastructure of the Internet expanded across the world, it did not develop in the same way everywhere. The cables, routers, and protocols were global, but the way people gained access to them depended heavily on national decisions, economic structures, and social priorities.

Two countries illustrate this difference well: Sweden and the United States.

They both had early access to the Internet. They both had strong technology sectors. But the way their populations connected to the network, and how quickly they did so, followed very different paths.

Sweden: The Internet as Public Infrastructure

In Sweden, the spread of the Internet was treated less as a commercial product and more as a societal project.

In the 1990s, the Swedish government introduced a policy known as the Home PC Reform. This allowed employees to purchase personal computers through their workplace using tax deductions. The goal was simple: increase computer literacy across the population.

The effect was immediate. Large numbers of households that previously had no computer suddenly had one. This created a foundation for widespread Internet adoption.

At the same time, Sweden began investing early in broadband infrastructure. Unlike traditional telephone-based connections, broadband allowed continuous, high-speed access to the Internet. Municipal networks, housing associations, and private companies all played a role in building out this infrastructure.

In some parts of Sweden, particularly in student housing and newly built residential areas, high-speed connections appeared surprisingly early. Already in the mid-1990s, certain housing projects provided Ethernet connections with speeds of 10 megabits per second directly to apartments. The Internet was something like a mirage to a young boy like me before my own home was connected, you could see the water in the desert. You wanted to quench your thirst for knowledge and entertainment. I remember the day when we got connected to the 10 megabit line as it was yesterday, I remember the smell of the cable as I broke the packaging and plugged it into the wall socket, and then the PC. And there it was, the world at the tip of my finger.

To understand how unusual this was, it helps to compare it to the typical experience in other countries at the time.

In the late 1990s and early 2000s, many people elsewhere were still using dial-up connections over telephone lines, often limited to speeds of around 56 kilobits per second. A 10 megabit connection was not just faster. It was hundreds of times faster.

This difference was not only technical. It changed how people used the Internet.

A slow connection encourages short, deliberate actions: checking email, loading a single webpage, disconnecting afterward. A fast, always-on connection encourages continuous use: downloading files, streaming media, participating in online communities, and leaving applications running in the background.

Another important factor in Sweden was how infrastructure was built.

Instead of relying entirely on a single national provider, multiple actors participated: municipal networks, housing cooperatives, private broadband companies and national telecom operators.

This created competition not only in pricing, but in technology. Companies experimented with fiber, cable, and early forms of high-speed DSL. In some cases, entire apartment complexes were wired directly with fiber or high-speed Ethernet.

The result was that Sweden moved relatively quickly toward broadband-based access, rather than remaining dependent on older telephone infrastructure.

By the early 2000s, broadband was becoming common, and adoption continued to accelerate. By 2010, around 92 percent of the Swedish population was using the Internet, one of the highest rates in the world.

The result of early unrestricted Internet access

Early access to high-speed Internet connections did not only change how people consumed information. It also changed how they produced, distributed, and thought about digital content.

Because many users had fast, always-on connections at home, Sweden became one of the most active environments for peer-to-peer file sharing in the early 2000s. This was not only a technical phenomenon. It was also cultural.

Peer-to-Peer Networks and Distributed Exchange

Peer-to-peer networks, often abbreviated as P2P, operate differently from traditional client-server systems.

Instead of downloading files from a central server, users connect directly to each other. Each participant in the network can both download and upload data at the same time. In effect, every user becomes part of the infrastructure.

Early systems such as Napster introduced the basic idea, but later networks removed central points of control. Protocols like BitTorrent allowed files to be split into many small pieces and distributed across thousands of users. A person downloading a file would receive pieces from multiple sources simultaneously while also sharing the parts they already had with others.

This made the system efficient, scalable, and difficult to shut down.

In countries with slower connections, this model worked but was limited. In Sweden, where broadband connections were relatively fast and stable, it worked exceptionally well.

Large files that would take many hours or days to download elsewhere could be transferred much more quickly. This made Sweden an ideal environment for large-scale file sharing.

The Emergence of a Sharing Culture

The technical conditions created a specific kind of culture.

File sharing in Sweden was not always seen primarily as a form of piracy. For many users, it was understood as a natural extension of how the Internet worked. If data could be copied without loss, and if networks allowed direct exchange between individuals, then sharing became an expected behavior.

As a result, large communities formed around sharing music, films, software, and other digital media.

Private trackers and invitation-only communities developed their own internal rules, economies, and reputations. Users were often required to maintain a certain upload-to-download ratio, encouraging them to contribute bandwidth back to the network rather than only consuming content.

In this way, file sharing networks were not chaotic systems. They were structured environments with their own forms of governance.

The Pirate Bay and Infrastructure as Ideology

One of the most well-known outcomes of this environment was the creation of The Pirate Bay.

Founded in 2003 by a group associated with the Swedish organization Piratbyrån, The Pirate Bay did not host copyrighted files directly. Instead, it provided a searchable index of torrent files, which allowed users to find and connect to peer-to-peer swarms.

Technically, this made it a coordination point rather than a storage system.

Culturally, it became something more.

The Pirate Bay presented itself not only as a service, but as a statement. It challenged existing models of copyright enforcement and raised questions about ownership in a digital environment where copying is trivial.

Legal actions against The Pirate Bay throughout the 2000s brought international attention to Sweden's file-sharing culture. Court cases, raids, and public debates turned what might have remained a technical subculture into a widely discussed political issue.

Out of this environment emerged the Swedish Pirate Party, which advocated for changes to copyright law, privacy protections, and digital rights.

Always-On Networks and the Normalization of Distribution

One of the less visible but more important factors behind this development was the nature of the connection itself.

In many Swedish households, Internet connections were fast and not metered by usage time

This allowed users to leave file-sharing programs running continuously.

A computer could remain connected to a peer-to-peer network for hours or days, uploading and downloading in the background. Over time, this created a persistent distributed system made up of thousands of home computers.

In contrast, in regions where connections were slower, unstable, or usage-based, this type of continuous participation was less common.

Early Hacking Communities and Technical Exploration

Alongside file sharing, Sweden also developed active communities interested in exploring and modifying computer systems.

The term "hacker" in this context did not always refer to criminal activity. It often described individuals who were deeply curious about how systems worked and how they could be altered or improved.

These communities existed in various forms such as bulletin board systems (BBS), IRC channels, small local networks and early online forums.

Participants shared knowledge about: operating systems, network protocols, software vulnerabilities and also hardware modification.

Some of this activity crossed into legally questionable areas, such as unauthorized access to systems or the distribution of cracked software. But much of it was driven by experimentation and learning.

Access to fast Internet connections made it easier to exchange tools, documentation, and large software packages. It also allowed real-time collaboration across distances.

Blurring the Line Between User and Infrastructure

One of the key outcomes of these developments was a shift in how users related to the Internet.

In a traditional model, users consume content from centralized services.

In the peer-to-peer model, users become part of the system itself.

A computer running a BitTorrent client is not just receiving data. It is also distributing it. A user participating in a file-sharing network contributes storage, bandwidth, and availability.

In Sweden, this model became normalized earlier than in many other places.

Legal and Political Reactions

As file sharing grew, it attracted attention from governments and industry organizations.

Media companies argued that widespread unauthorized distribution of copyrighted material threatened existing business models. Legal frameworks that had been developed for physical media were applied to digital distribution, often with difficulty.

Sweden became a focal point for these conflicts.

Police raids, court cases, and international pressure highlighted the tension between the technical possibilities, legal systems and cultural attitudes toward information sharing

The outcome was not a simple resolution, but an ongoing negotiation between these forces.

A Precursor to Later Developments

The file-sharing and hacker culture that emerged in Sweden during this period can be seen as an early example of broader patterns that would later define the Internet.

Many of the dynamics that would later appear in social media, streaming platforms, and online communities were already present in these early environments.

The Internet was no longer just a network of machines. It had become a space where technical systems, human behavior, and questions of control began to interact in complex ways.

And in places where the infrastructure allowed it, those interactions happened earlier, faster, and at a larger scale.

The United States: The Internet as a Commercial Service

In the United States, the development followed a different model.

The early Internet itself had been created there, but its transition into a public service was largely driven by private companies. Telecommunications infrastructure was already dominated by large operators, and Internet access became one more service layered on top of existing systems.

For many households, the first experience of the Internet came through dial-up connections using the same copper telephone lines used for voice calls. These connections were slow and temporary. Users would connect, use the Internet, and then disconnect, often paying per minute or tying up the household phone line.

Broadband began to appear in the late 1990s and early 2000s, mainly through two technologies: DSL (which used existing telephone lines) & cable Internet (which used television networks).

However, unlike in Sweden, the roll-out of broadband in the United States was uneven.

In densely populated urban areas, faster connections became available relatively quickly. But in suburban and rural areas, older infrastructure remained in place for much longer. Because DSL depended on the quality and distance of telephone lines, speeds varied widely and often remained limited.

Even into the 2010s, many parts of the United States still relied on DSL connections with relatively low speeds compared to fiber-based networks. While newer technologies existed, they were not deployed uniformly across the country.

This created a fragmented experience of the Internet.

Some users had fast, always-on broadband connections. Others still experienced the Internet as slow, unstable, or limited.

The limits of access and the rise of platforms

Limited and uneven access to high-speed Internet did not only affect how quickly people could download information. It also shaped the structure of the Internet itself.

In many parts of the United States, especially outside major cities, Internet connections remained constrained well into the 2000s and even the 2010s. DSL connections depended heavily on distance from telephone exchanges, and speeds could drop significantly over relatively short distances. Cable connections were often faster, but they were shared among neighborhoods and could slow down during peak usage times.

Another important limitation was asymmetry.

Most consumer Internet connections in the United States were designed with much higher download speeds than upload speeds. A typical connection might allow a user to receive data relatively quickly, but sending data back to the network was much slower.

This had an important consequence.

It made the Internet easier to consume than to contribute to.

Uploading large files, hosting services from home, or participating in distributed systems like peer-to-peer networks was technically possible, but often inefficient or unreliable for many users. While file sharing did exist in the United States, the infrastructure did not support it as naturally or as efficiently as in regions with faster and more symmetrical connections.

Instead, a different model became dominant.

From distribution to centralization

Because individual users were limited in their ability to upload and distribute data, content increasingly became concentrated in centralized locations.

Rather than users exchanging files directly with each other, data was hosted on dedicated servers with high-bandwidth connections. These servers were located in data centers operated by companies that could afford the necessary infrastructure.

This result was a pattern: users downloaded from centralized sources, companies hosted and distributed content and the infrastructure became concentrated in fewer locations.

Over time, this model became the default.

Websites, online services, and later platforms acted as central points where information was stored and accessed. Instead of a distributed network of participants sharing data with each other, the Internet in practice began to resemble a system where many users connected to a smaller number of powerful nodes.

The emergence of platform-based services

This structure created the conditions for the rise of platforms.

When users are primarily consuming rather than distributing, services naturally evolve to organize, host, and deliver content at scale. Companies began building systems that aggregated content and made it easily accessible through centralized interfaces.

Early examples included:

- large web hosting providers
- content portals
- streaming services

These systems solved real technical problems. They provided:

- reliability
- speed
- ease of use

But they also introduced a new dynamic.

Control over infrastructure increasingly meant control over access.

A platform that hosts content can:

- decide what is visible
- prioritize certain types of information
- remove or restrict access

This was not necessarily the result of a single decision. It emerged gradually from the interaction between technical limitations and economic incentives.

Infrastructure as a constraint on behavior

The difference between Sweden and the United States during this period illustrates a broader principle.

People tend to use the Internet in ways that their connections allow.

In Sweden, fast and symmetrical connections made it practical for users to:

- share large amounts of data
- run services from home
- participate in distributed systems

In the United States, slower upload speeds and uneven access made it more practical to:

- consume content from centralized sources
- rely on hosted services
- interact within controlled environments

The result was not just a difference in speed, but a difference in structure.

One environment encouraged participation in the network itself. The other encouraged interaction with services built on top of it.

The beginning of a new model

By the early 2010s, this pattern had become more pronounced.

Even as faster connections became available in parts of the United States, the underlying structure remained.

Users were no longer primarily exchanging data directly with each other. Instead, they were interacting through platforms that mediated nearly every activity:

- communication
- media consumption
- information access

This model would go on to define much of the modern Internet.

It did not replace the earlier, more distributed forms entirely. But it became dominant in many regions, shaping how billions of people experienced the network.

Speed as a Cultural Factor

The difference in infrastructure led not only to differences in speed, but to entirely different ways of using the Internet.

In Sweden, early access to high-speed connections encouraged:

- large file sharing
- online gaming
- continuous Internet use
- early adoption of streaming and digital services

In the United States, slower and less consistent access meant that many of these behaviors developed later or unevenly.

A user with a slow connection sees the Internet as something to access occasionally. A user with a fast connection sees it as an environment they are always inside.

Early High-Speed Culture

In Sweden and other early broadband countries, this environment produced new forms of digital culture.

File sharing became widespread, particularly with the rise of peer-to-peer networks. Services like Kazaa and later BitTorrent allowed users to exchange large files directly with each other. Sweden became one of the central locations for this activity, both technically and culturally.

Online gaming also expanded rapidly. With low latency connections, players could interact in real time across long distances. Communities formed around games, forums, and early social platforms.

Because many users had fast connections at home, the Internet was not limited to workplaces or universities. It became embedded in everyday life.

Infrastructure Shapes Society

The comparison between Sweden and the United States reveals a broader pattern.

The Internet is often described as a global system, but access to it is always local.

It depends on:

- government policy
- economic incentives
- geography
- existing infrastructure

These factors determine:

- who gets access

- how fast that access is
- how stable the connection is
- and ultimately, how the Internet is used

In Sweden, coordinated policy, early investment, and competition led to widespread high-speed access relatively early.

In the United States, market-driven deployment created a more uneven landscape, where access and speed varied significantly depending on location.

The Beginning of Divergence

By the early 2000s, the Internet was no longer a single shared experience.

It had already begun to diverge into different forms depending on where and how people connected.

Some users experienced a fast, always-on network that supported constant interaction and large-scale data exchange.

Others experienced a slower, more limited version of the same system.

This divergence would continue to shape everything that came next:

- how platforms developed
- how content spread
- how online communities formed
- and how power emerged on the Internet

The physical network was global, but the experience of using it was not.

And from this point forward, those differences would begin to matter more and more.

B
BAHNHOF

Image showing the entrance to "Pionen"

Pionen is a highly secure underground data center located in Stockholm, operated by the Swedish company Bahnhof. Built inside a former Cold War nuclear bunker, it sits about 30 meters below ground and is designed to withstand extreme conditions.

The facility is known for its distinctive, almost sci-fi interior. The servers are housed within raw rock chambers, with reinforced doors, backup power systems, and advanced cooling. Its design emphasizes both security and reliability, protecting critical data infrastructure from physical threats.

Pionen gained international attention because it once hosted servers for The Pirate Bay. This made it a symbol of digital freedom and controversy, as the site was at the center of global debates about copyright and online file sharing.

Today, Pionen continues to operate as a secure data center, representing the physical backbone of the internet, hidden underground, yet essential to keeping digital services running.

Image showing part of the futuristic interior to "Pionen"

Pionen is a highly secure underground data center located in Stockholm, operated by the Swedish company Bahnhof. Built inside a former Cold War nuclear bunker, it sits about 30 meters below ground and is designed to withstand extreme conditions.

The facility is known for its distinctive, almost sci-fi interior. The servers are housed within raw rock chambers, with reinforced doors, backup power systems, and advanced cooling. Its design emphasizes both security and reliability, protecting critical data infrastructure from physical threats.

Pionen gained international attention because it once hosted servers for The Pirate Bay. This made it a symbol of digital freedom and controversy, as the site was at the center of global debates about copyright and online file sharing.

Today, Pionen continues to operate as a secure data center, representing the physical backbone of the internet, hidden underground, yet essential to keeping digital services running.

intel
Core 2

Sweden Jönköping - Dreamhack Lanparty winter 2007 D-hall, view to mainstage. Dreamhack was considered the world's largest LAN party at the time. It gathered thousands of participants (over 10,000 computers connected) in one venue

Photo by Martin from Tyrol, via Wikimedia Commons (CC BY-SA 2.0)

"Sweden Jönköping – DreamHack Lanparty Winter 2007" by Martin from Tyrol, via Wikimedia Commons, CC BY-SA 2.0

Chapter 4 – Before the Web: The First Connected Public

Before continuing forward, it is necessary to step back in time.

In the previous chapters, we moved quickly through different stages of the Internet's development. We began with its physical origins, followed its expansion across continents, and then examined how different societies adopted and used it at scale. In doing so, we briefly entered a period where the Internet was already fast, widespread, and integrated into everyday life.

But this was not how the Internet first appeared to the public.

To understand how people originally experienced digital networks, we need to return to an earlier stage, before broadband, before always-on connections, and before large platforms. This chapter focuses on the period between roughly the early 1980s and the early 2000s, when individuals began connecting from their homes using systems that were often slow, fragmented, and experimental.

This was the first time that ordinary people, not just universities or institutions, could participate in networked communication. The systems they used were different from the modern Internet in both structure and experience, but many of the behaviors, cultures, and ideas that define the Internet today began to take shape during this period.

Before the Internet became a seamless, always-on system used by billions of people, it existed as a collection of smaller, fragmented networks used by individuals connecting from their homes. These early systems were not unified, not standardized, and often not permanent. They were built by enthusiasts, operated on personal machines, and accessed through telephone lines. Yet within these limitations, something new began to emerge. For the first time, ordinary people could communicate, share information, and form communities across distance without relying on traditional institutions.

The experience of connecting to these early systems was very different from what we now think of as the Internet. It required intention. It required patience. And it required a certain level of technical understanding. But it also created a sense of discovery that is difficult to replicate in a more polished and centralized network.

Usenet: A Distributed Conversation

One of the earliest systems that allowed people to communicate across networks was Usenet.

Usenet began in the late 1970s and allowed messages to be shared across multiple servers. Instead of connecting to a single machine, users connected to a server that was part of a larger network. Messages posted on one server would propagate to others, creating a shared space for discussion.

These discussions were organized into groups based on topics, such as technology, science, politics, or hobbies. Anyone with access to a Usenet server could read and contribute to these conversations.

Unlike modern platforms, there was no central authority controlling Usenet as a whole. Each server was independently operated, and administrators could choose which groups to carry or how to moderate them. This created a system that was both decentralized and loosely coordinated.

Usenet still exists today, although it is no longer widely used by the general public. It continues to operate through a network of servers that exchange messages using standardized protocols. Access is typically provided by specialized service providers or through Internet service providers that still maintain Usenet servers.

Modern usage of Usenet falls into two main categories. Some users participate in discussions, particularly in long-standing technical or niche communities. Others use it for file distribution, where large amounts of data are stored and shared across servers. In this form, Usenet functions less like a discussion system and more like a distributed storage network.

Because of its decentralized nature and long history, Usenet represents one of the earliest examples of a large-scale online community that still persists in a recognizable form.

Bulletin Board Systems: Small Worlds on Telephone Lines

Around the same time as Usenet in the late 1970s and early 1980s, a different kind of system began to appear: Bulletin Board Systems.
These systems, often called BBSes, became one of the earliest ways for individuals to connect with each other digitally.

A BBS was typically a single computer, often located in someone's home, connected to a telephone line through a modem. To access it, a user would dial the phone number of that machine. If the line was free, they would connect directly to that computer. If someone else was already connected, they would hear a busy signal and have to try again later.

This meant that each BBS was a small, self-contained world. It had its own users, its own rules, and its own culture. The person running the system, known as the system operator or "sysop," had complete control over how it functioned. They decided who could join, what could be shared, and how the system was organized.

Inside a BBS, users could leave messages for each other, participate in discussions, and download or upload files. Some systems specialized in particular interests, such as programming, gaming, or music. Others were more general, acting as local community hubs.

Because these systems were often limited to one or a few simultaneous connections, they created a very different kind of interaction. Conversations were slower. Messages might be left hours or days apart. But they were also more deliberate.

Although most BBS systems disappeared as the Internet became more widespread, some still exist today. Enthusiasts continue to operate them, often preserving the original experience as closely as possible. Modern users can connect either through traditional dial-up methods, where available, or through Internet-based connections that simulate the original process. These systems are used by hobbyists, historians, and individuals interested in preserving early digital culture.

Dial-Up Connections: The Sound of Access

Throughout the 1980s and into the 1990s, most of these systems were accessed using dial-up connections.

Accessing early networks required a modem, a device that converted digital signals into sounds that could travel over telephone lines.

Connecting involved dialing a number and waiting as the modem established a link. This process produced a series of distinctive tones and static-like noises, which became one of the defining sensory experiences of early Internet use.

The connection was temporary. When a user connected, the telephone line was occupied. This meant that no one else in the household could use the phone at the same time. In many cases, users were also charged based on how long they stayed connected. I was around for this era of the internet, this was my first experience with internet, I could only be online for a short period at a time because it was very expensive, and as mentioned the phone line would be blocked. Since cellphones were not a common thing in those times it was a big deal to block the phone connection to the home. I still remember the sound of the modem by heart, to this day I still hear it in my thoughts sometimes, you really felt that you connected to something bigger. You never hear “analogue“ sounds like that anymore.

These constraints shaped behavior. People planned what they wanted to do before connecting. They downloaded messages or files, disconnected, and then read or interacted with them offline. The Internet was not something you were always inside. It was something you visited.

Even today, dial-up connections have not completely disappeared. In some remote areas, they are still used as a fallback where broadband infrastructure is unavailable. There are also communities that maintain dial-up systems for historical or experimental purposes, preserving not only the technology but the experience of using it.

IRC: Real-Time Global Communication

If Usenet was slow and asynchronous, Internet Relay Chat, or IRC, introduced real-time communication.

For many users, this was the first time communication on the Internet felt immediate rather than delayed.

IRC allowed users to connect to servers and join channels where they could exchange messages instantly with others around the world. Unlike BBS systems, which were often local, IRC was inherently global.

Users identified themselves with nicknames rather than real names. These identities could be temporary or persistent, and they were not tied to any formal verification system. This allowed for a level of anonymity and flexibility that was uncommon in traditional communication systems.

Conversations took place inside channels, which were organized around interests, communities, or specific topics. Some were open to anyone. Others were private or required invitations. Within these spaces, users could communicate in real time, with messages appearing instantly as others typed.

Unlike modern messaging platforms, IRC was minimal in design. There were no profiles, no images, and no built-in recommendation systems. Users needed to know which server to connect to and which channels to join. This made the experience less guided, but also more direct.

Channels could range from casual conversation to highly technical discussion. Many early Internet users relied on IRC to ask questions, share knowledge, and collaborate across distances. It also became an important tool for coordination, particularly in communities involved in software development, file sharing, and other collaborative activities.

IRC is still in use today, although it has been largely replaced in mainstream use by messaging platforms and social media. It remains popular among certain groups, particularly in technical communities and open-source projects, as well as among users who value its simplicity and decentralized nature.

Because IRC does not rely on a single central service, it continues to operate as a network of independent servers. Anyone with the necessary knowledge can run a server or connect to an existing one. This allows it to persist as a form of communication that remains closely aligned with the original design of the Internet.

Early File Sharing and the Origins of Distribution Networks

As these early systems grew through the 1980s and early 1990s, new forms of file sharing began to emerge. Unlike the modern Internet, where large files can be transferred almost instantly, early file sharing existed within strict technical limits. Connections were slow, storage was scarce, and networks were fragmented. These constraints did not prevent distribution, but they shaped how it developed.

On Bulletin Board Systems, file sharing was handled directly by the host machine. A user would connect, browse available files, and download what they needed. In some cases, they could also upload files for others to access. Because each system had limited storage and bandwidth, the availability of files was often carefully managed. System operators decided what could remain on the system, and popular files were sometimes removed to make space for new ones.

Despite these limitations, users began to move files between systems in increasingly organized ways. A file uploaded to one BBS did not necessarily stay there. It could be downloaded, carried to another system, and uploaded again, slowly spreading across a network of independent machines. This process was not automated. It relied on individuals who were willing to spend time transferring data from place to place.

Out of this environment, more structured forms of distribution began to take shape.

One of the most influential developments during this period was the emergence of organized groups dedicated to distributing software and other digital material. These groups, often referred to collectively as "the scene," began forming in the 1980s and became more structured over time.

A typical scene group operated with a clear internal organization. Members specialized in different roles. Some focused on obtaining new software, sometimes before it was widely available. Others worked on modifying or packaging it, which could include removing copy protection or preparing it for easier distribution. Once ready, the release would be given a name and distributed under the group's identity.

Distribution itself followed specific paths. Files would move between systems through networks of trusted users, sometimes called couriers, who transferred data from one location to another. Certain systems acted as central hubs, receiving new releases and then passing them along. Speed became important. Groups competed to release material faster than others, and reputation was built on how quickly and reliably they could distribute new content.

Because connections were slow, efficiency became essential. Files were compressed to reduce their size and often split into multiple parts. A user would download each part separately and then reconstruct the original file on their own system. These practices became standard and would later appear in more advanced file-sharing systems.

At the same time, other methods of file distribution were developing alongside BBS networks.

File Transfer Protocol, or FTP, introduced a more direct way to store and access files over network connections. Unlike BBS systems, which were often accessed through dial-up telephone lines, FTP servers were connected to early Internet infrastructure and could serve multiple users at once. Universities, research institutions, and later private operators ran FTP servers that allowed users to upload and download files from centralized locations.

Some of these servers became large repositories of software, documents, and other digital material. Access was sometimes public, but in many cases it was restricted. Private FTP servers, often referred to as "FTP sites," were used by more organized groups, including those involved in software distribution. These servers offered higher speeds and more storage than most BBS systems, making them valuable points in the distribution network.

Usenet also became a method of file sharing, even though it had originally been designed for text-based discussion. Because the system was built to distribute messages, users found ways to encode binary files into text formats that could be posted and propagated across servers. These encoded files would then be downloaded and reconstructed by other users. This allowed files to spread across a distributed network without relying on a single central server.

Across these systems, a pattern began to emerge. File sharing was no longer limited to a single machine or a local community. It was becoming a networked activity, involving multiple systems, coordinated distribution paths, and communities of users who contributed to the process.

Although these methods were slow and often complex, they established many of the principles that would later define the Internet. They demonstrated that digital information could be copied without loss and distributed widely without centralized control. They also showed that users were not only consumers of information, but active participants in its movement.

As connections improved in the late 1990s and early 2000s, these existing practices did not disappear. Instead, they expanded.

Systems like Napster and later BitTorrent did not invent file sharing. They simplified and accelerated processes that had already been developing for decades. What had once required coordinated effort across multiple systems could now happen automatically between users.

In regions where high-speed connections became available early, these new systems could operate at a much larger scale. The patterns that had formed slowly on BBS networks, FTP servers, and Usenet began to evolve into continuous, large-scale distribution systems.

In countries like Sweden, where fast and stable connections were introduced earlier than in many other places, these developments took on a different character. The technical limitations that had previously constrained file sharing were reduced, allowing users to participate more directly and continuously in the distribution process.

The result was not a completely new phenomenon, but an acceleration of something that had already been taking shape for years.

What appeared to be a sudden shift toward large-scale file sharing was, in reality, the continuation of earlier systems, adapted to a new level of connectivity.

The Early Web and Personal Publishing

As the Internet became more standardized in the early to mid-1990s, the World Wide Web introduced a new way of sharing information.

Unlike earlier systems such as BBS networks or Usenet, which required specific software or knowledge of particular servers, the web provided a more uniform interface. Users could access information through web browsers, navigating between pages using links. This made the Internet more accessible to a wider audience, even for those without deep technical knowledge.

Early websites were simple in structure. Most consisted of static pages written in basic HTML, often containing text, simple layouts, and low-resolution images. There were no dynamic feeds, no personalized content, and no large-scale platforms organizing information. Each site existed as its own independent space.

Many of these sites were created by individuals rather than organizations. Personal homepages became common, where users shared information about themselves, their interests, and their projects. These pages often included collections of links, small pieces of writing, or curated resources. In many cases, they served as both identity and expression, allowing users to present themselves in a way that was not mediated by any central system.

This period saw the emergence of a culture of self-publishing. Anyone with access to a server and some basic technical knowledge could create a website and make it available to others. Publishing on the Internet did not require approval, distribution networks, or institutional backing. It was enough to create a page and make it accessible.

Mailing lists and newsletters also played an important role during this time. Instead of visiting a website repeatedly, users could subscribe to receive messages directly in their inbox. These systems allowed communities to form around shared interests, with discussions and information distributed to groups of subscribers. In some ways, they combined elements of earlier systems such as Usenet with the growing accessibility of the web.

Navigation during this period was often manual and exploratory. Search engines existed but were limited, and much of the web was discovered through directories, shared links, or recommendations from other users. Moving through the web required a degree of curiosity and effort, similar to earlier systems.

Although the web introduced a more unified interface, it did not immediately replace earlier forms of communication and distribution. BBS systems, IRC, Usenet, and FTP servers continued to operate alongside it. Users often moved between these systems, using each for different purposes.

Over time, the web became the dominant interface through which most people accessed the Internet. Its simplicity and flexibility allowed it to grow rapidly, eventually absorbing many of the functions that had previously been handled by separate systems.

However, the early web remained fundamentally decentralized. Websites were independently created and maintained, and there was no single authority controlling how information was published or accessed.

Although the modern web has become more complex and increasingly centralized, these early forms of publishing still exist. Personal websites, blogs, and independent newsletters continue to be used by individuals who want to communicate directly without relying entirely on large platforms.

Fragmentation and Exploration

The early Internet was not a single, unified space. It was a collection of different systems, each with its own structure, access methods, and communities. To use it effectively, a person needed to know not only how to connect, but where to go.

Finding information was not automatic. There were no centralized search engines capable of indexing everything, and no platforms organizing content into a single interface. Instead, users had to rely on knowledge and experience. They needed to know the address of a system, be invited into certain communities, or learn specific commands and interfaces in order to access information.

This created a very different kind of interaction with the network.

Users did not passively receive content. They moved between systems, often with a clear intention, but also with a willingness to explore. New resources were discovered through shared directories, recommendations from other users, or simple curiosity. In many cases, access depended on trust or familiarity, particularly in more restricted systems.

Because the network was fragmented, no single system defined the experience. A user might read discussions on Usenet, connect to a BBS for files, use IRC for real-time communication, and access FTP servers or early websites for specific resources. Each system served a different purpose, and understanding how they fit together was part of using the Internet.

The effort required to navigate these systems shaped the culture that formed around them. Users developed technical skills, shared knowledge with each other, and often contributed to the systems they used. Participation was more active, and access was not always immediate.

At the same time, the lack of centralization meant that users had more direct control over how they interacted with the network. There were fewer intermediaries, fewer layers of abstraction, and fewer mechanisms guiding behavior. The Internet was not yet organized for convenience. It was something that had to be learned.

It Was A Different Kind of Internet (But still the same)

The early Internet was shaped by limitation, but those limitations created specific forms of behavior.

Connections were slow, so people were deliberate.
Systems were fragmented, so people explored.
Infrastructure was limited, so people built their own solutions.

As the Internet grew and became more accessible, many of these characteristics changed. Systems became faster, more integrated, and easier to use. But they also became more centralized.

The early forms of the Internet did not disappear entirely. They remain as a parallel layer beneath the modern network, still accessible to those who seek them out.

They represent an earlier version of what the Internet could be: a collection of systems where users were not only participants, but often builders, operators, and maintainers of the network itself.

What Still Remains

Many of the systems from this early period have not disappeared. They have become smaller, more specialized, or less visible, but they continue to operate quietly alongside the modern Internet.

Bulletin Board Systems still exist, often maintained by enthusiasts who preserve both the technology and the experience. Some of these systems can still be accessed in ways that closely resemble their original form. In certain cases, users connect through actual telephone lines using dial-up modems. More commonly today, connections are made over the Internet using software that simulates the older process. Despite the change in access method, the structure remains the same. A single system, operated by an individual, hosting its own community and files.

These systems are not widely used, but they are not inactive. They are maintained by hobbyists, historians, and individuals who value the direct control and simplicity they offer. In some cases, they function as living archives of early digital culture. In others, they continue to operate as small, active communities.

Usenet also continues to exist as a distributed network of servers exchanging messages. Although its role has changed, it has not disappeared. Some groups remain active for discussion, particularly in technical or long-standing communities. At the same time, Usenet is still used for large-scale file distribution. Unlike modern platforms, it operates without a single central authority, relying instead on independently operated servers that synchronize with each other. Access is typically provided through specialized providers, and while it is less visible to the general public, it remains a functioning part of the Internet.

Internet Relay Chat continues to host real-time communication in a similar way to how it did decades ago. Many open-source software projects still rely on IRC for coordination, and some communities prefer it for its simplicity and lack of central control. It remains a network of independent servers rather than a single platform, and users can still connect using basic clients with minimal requirements.

Dial-up connections, while largely obsolete for everyday use, have not completely disappeared. In some remote areas, they still function as a fallback when modern infrastructure is unavailable. There are also individuals and small communities that maintain dial-up access intentionally, either for preservation or experimentation. The experience remains fundamentally the same: a temporary connection established over a telephone line, limited in speed but direct in its operation.

File Transfer Protocol servers are still used as well, particularly in technical environments. While many have been replaced by web-based systems, FTP continues to exist as a simple and direct method for transferring files. Some public servers remain accessible, and private ones are still used for controlled distribution within organizations or communities.

Personal websites, independent blogs, and self-hosted services also continue to exist alongside large platforms. Although they are less dominant than in the early days of the web, they represent a continuation of the same idea: individuals publishing information directly, without relying entirely on centralized systems. In recent years, there has even been a renewed interest in these forms of publishing, as some users seek alternatives to platform-based communication.

What connects all of these systems is not just their age, but their structure.

They operate differently from most modern Internet services. They are often decentralized or loosely coordinated. They are typically maintained by individuals or small groups rather than large organizations. They require more effort to access and use, but in return they offer a different kind of control.

The people who continue to use these systems do so for different reasons. Some are interested in preservation, keeping older technologies and practices alive. Others value the independence these systems provide, where control is not concentrated in a single platform. In some cases, users are drawn to the transparency and simplicity of these systems, where the underlying structure is visible and understandable.

These parts of the Internet do not dominate the network anymore, but they have not been replaced entirely. They exist as a parallel layer, still accessible, still functioning, and still reflecting an earlier way of thinking about communication and distribution.

They show that the Internet did not evolve in a straight line. Older systems were not simply discarded. They were absorbed, reduced, or moved to the edges, but they remain part of the network.

And for those who know where to look, they are still there.

To understand how these systems were actually used, it is useful to look at the messages themselves.

The early Internet was not abstract. It was made up of discussions, questions, arguments, and attempts to define what this new form of communication should be. Much of this activity took place in public systems such as Usenet, where messages were distributed across networks and preserved over time.

Some of these messages still exist. They provide a direct glimpse into how people thought about the Internet while it was still forming.

As more people began to use the network in the early 1990s, there was a growing need to define how communication should work. In 1995, a document known as RFC 1855 attempted to formalize expected behavior online. Unlike many modern systems, these guidelines were not enforced by a platform, but shared as recommendations for users.

The following excerpts are drawn from publicly archived materials and are presented in shortened form for historical and illustrative purposes.

RFC 1855 - Netiquette Guidelines

October 1995

Remember that the person receiving your mail

is a human being whose culture, language,

and humor have different points of reference.

This shows an important characteristic of the early Internet. Behavior was not controlled by systems, but negotiated between users.

As access expanded, long-time participants began to notice changes in how these systems were used. One of the most well-known examples comes from a discussion on the Usenet newsgroup *alt.folklore.computers* in early 1994:

From: Dave Fischer

Newsgroups: alt.folklore.computers

Date: Jan 1994

It's moot now. September 1993 will go down in net.history

as the September that never ended.

This message referred to what became known as “Eternal September.”

Before this period, new users typically arrived in predictable cycles, often at the start of academic terms. Over time, these users would learn the norms of the system. In 1993, this pattern changed. Large numbers of new users began arriving continuously through commercial Internet providers, and the process of adaptation no longer stabilized.

The scale of access had begun to change the nature of the network itself.

Other users in the same discussion reflected similar observations:

```
From: Joel Furr

Newsgroups: alt.folklore.computers

Date: Jan 8, 1994

Is it just me, or has Delphi unleashed a staggering

amount of weirdos on the net?
From: Karl Reinsch

Newsgroups: alt.folklore.computers

Date: Jan 8, 1994

Of course it's perpetually September for Delphi users,

isn't it?
```

These messages show how the expansion of access was experienced in real time. What had once been smaller, more self-regulating communities began to change as new users arrived in large numbers.

At the same time, not all communication on the early Internet was structured or easy to interpret. Some messages became well-known simply because they were unusual.

One example appeared on Usenet in 1996, in a post that later became known as "Markovian Parallax Denigrate." (*see page 56 for more information*)

Markovian Parallax Denigrate Post from 1996:

Subject: Markovian parallax denigrate

Date: Aug 5, 1996

jitterbugging McKinley Abe break Newtonian inferring

caw update Cohen air collaborate rue sportswriting

rococo invocate tousle shadflower

The meaning of this message was never clearly established. It is often cited as an example of the unpredictable and sometimes opaque nature of early online communication.

Taken together, these fragments show a network that was still being defined by its users. There was no single authority determining how communication should work, no unified interface, and no consistent experience.

Instead, the Internet existed as a collection of conversations, shaped in real time by the people participating in them.

Alongside public discussions on systems like Usenet, other forms of communication and distribution developed in less visible parts of the network. These systems were often more fragmented, more technical, and in some cases intentionally private. They included bulletin board systems dedicated to file distribution, organized release groups, and early mailing lists where technical and philosophical ideas were discussed in depth. While less visible, these systems played an important role in shaping how the Internet was used.

By the late 1980s and early 1990s, organized groups had formed around the distribution of software. These groups, often referred to as "the scene," developed structured methods for releasing and spreading files across networks. Each release typically included a text file describing the group, the release, and any relevant notes. These files were distributed alongside the software itself and became a defining feature of scene culture. They established identity, reputation, and continuity within a distributed system where no central authority existed.

Much of this activity involved software piracy, with groups distributing cracked programs or games for free. However, these groups represented the upper echelon of that ecosystem, operating with a high degree of organization, technical skill, and internal standards.

At the same time, bulletin board systems hosted large collections of text files, often referred to simply as "textfiles." These documents covered a wide range of topics, including programming, hacking, telecommunications, and general exploration of computer systems. Some were instructional, others speculative, and many reflected a strong sense of curiosity about how systems worked. They were copied between systems, shared across networks, and gradually formed a distributed archive of knowledge.

`The system is only as secure as the people running it.`

`Most of what is called "hacking" is not breaking systems,`

`but understanding them better than the people who built them.`

`Information is the most valuable resource on any network.`

As the Internet expanded in the early 1990s, discussions about privacy and control began to take on greater importance. One of the most influential spaces for these discussions was the cypherpunk mailing list, where programmers, researchers, and activists explored how cryptography could be used to protect communication and individual autonomy.A widely cited statement from this environment appeared in 1993:

`Privacy is necessary for an open society in the electronic age.`

This line, taken from what became known as the Cypherpunk Manifesto, reflected a growing awareness that the structure of the Internet would influence not only how information moved, but how power and control would be distributed.

These systems operated alongside the more visible parts of the Internet, but followed different principles. They were often decentralized, loosely coordinated, and maintained by individuals or small groups. Participation required knowledge and effort, and access was not always open.

At the same time, they demonstrated alternative ways of organizing communication and distribution. File sharing networks, privacy-focused communication, and user-driven systems were already being explored in these environments, long before they became widely adopted.

They formed a parallel layer of the Internet, less visible but deeply influential, where many of the ideas that would later shape the network were first tested in practice.

Bulletin board systems did not only host conversations and files. They also became repositories for text documents that circulated across networks, copied from system to system and preserved by users. Many of these textfiles were written anonymously or under pseudonyms, and they reflected a mixture of technical curiosity, experimentation, and attempts to understand the systems that were emerging.

Some of these textfiles were simple guides. Others were reflections on technology, security, and the structure of networks themselves. Because they were distributed freely and repeatedly copied, many of them became widely available through public archives.

The following excerpt reflects the tone found in widely circulated BBS textfiles:

`Hacking is not about breaking into systems.`

`It is about understanding them.`

Texts like this were not formal publications. They were copied, modified, and shared repeatedly, often without attribution. Over time, they became part of a distributed body of knowledge that existed outside of traditional publishing systems.

Alongside these textfiles, another form of communication developed within software distribution networks. These were known as NFO files.

An NFO file was a plain text document included with a software release. It identified the group responsible for the release, described what had been done to the software, and communicated with other groups or users. Because early systems were entirely text-based, these files often included visual elements created using ASCII characters. These designs functioned as logos, giving each group a recognizable identity across different systems.

The following excerpt is taken from a preserved scene release file from the early 1990s:

`RAZOR 1911 PROUDLY PRESENTS`

`Protection removed.`

`Packed and tested.`

`Greets to all groups keeping the scene alive.`

These files were not only technical notes. They were a form of communication between groups that rarely interacted directly. Through these messages, groups established reputation, acknowledged each other, and maintained continuity within a decentralized network.

For many users, these files were the first thing they saw. Before running the software, they encountered the group that had released it, the message it carried, and the structure of the network behind it.

At the same time, more formal publications also emerged within these networks. One of the most well-known was *Phrack*, an underground digital magazine focused on hacking, telecommunications, and computer systems. First published in 1985, it was distributed through BBS systems and later across the Internet.

The following excerpt comes from the introduction to an early issue of Phrack:

`Welcome to Phrack Inc.`

`The following textfiles are for informational purposes only.`

`We do not condone the use of this information for illegal activities.`

Phrack combined technical writing with a strong sense of identity and culture. It existed outside traditional publishing systems, yet it reached a global audience through the networks that connected these communities.

Both textfiles, NFO files, and publications like Phrack reflect a particular moment in the development of the Internet. They show a network where users were not only consuming information, but actively producing, shaping, and distributing it.

These systems were limited, but within those limits, new forms of communication and expression emerged. They were not centrally organized or controlled. Instead, they were maintained by the people who used them.

Many of these artifacts remain preserved today, not because they were formally archived, but because they were copied, shared, and valued within the network itself.

Chapter 5 – The Eerie and Unsettling

The Dark Side of the Early Internet

Alongside the curiosity, experimentation, and collaboration that defined the early Internet, there was another side that developed in parallel. It was less visible, less structured, and often deliberately unsettling. In the same networks that hosted technical discussions and academic exchange, there also circulated files that focused on shock, taboo, and the boundaries of what could be expressed in a digital space.

These files appeared in many forms. Some were written as guides, describing extreme or disturbing acts in a detached, instructional tone. Others were framed as confessions or first-person accounts, presenting themselves as real experiences involving violence, cannibalism, or other forms of transgressive behavior. There were also documents that claimed to reveal hidden knowledge, conspiracies, or secret systems operating behind the visible world. A recurring category within these were files that claimed to document brainwashing techniques, secret experiments, or methods of psychological manipulation. These texts often presented themselves with a tone of authority, mimicking scientific reports or classified documents. In some cases, they were loosely inspired by real historical programs or fragments of declassified material, but heavily distorted, exaggerated, or entirely fictionalized in their content.

Among the most unsettling of these were so-called "shock files," which circulated widely across BBS systems and early Internet archives. One of the most infamous types took the form of cooking-style documents that described the preparation of human flesh in the language of a recipe. These texts were written in a disturbingly calm and methodical tone, often imitating the structure of ordinary cookbooks. Whether intended as satire, provocation, or something else entirely, they created a strong reaction in those who encountered them. What made them particularly disturbing was not only their content, but the uncertainty surrounding them. There have been real, documented cases of cannibalism throughout history, and because these files were anonymous and unverifiable, it was impossible to know whether they were purely fictional or loosely inspired by real events. Even if they were intended as shock fiction, the ambiguity itself contributed to their impact.

Other files followed similar patterns. Some presented themselves as guides to becoming a hitman, describing methods, rules, and procedures in a tone that resembled technical documentation. Others claimed to reveal interrogation techniques, psychological conditioning methods, or secret government practices. There were also texts written as if they were recovered documents, incomplete fragments of larger systems, or instructions that assumed knowledge the reader did not have. Many of these shared a common structure: they blurred the line between reality and fiction, using familiar formats to make their content feel more credible.

A particularly distinctive category consisted of text files that combined ASCII art with narrative writing. Because early systems were limited to plain text, visual elements had to be constructed from characters. This led to the creation of elaborate images, symbols, and patterns embedded directly into the text. Around these visuals, authors would build narratives that often resembled rituals, instructions, or fragments of obscure belief systems. Some of these texts mimicked religious or occult language, presenting sequences of actions or symbols as if they carried meaning or power. Others leaned into horror, describing events or entities in a way that felt intentionally disorienting or disturbing. In some cases, the text would appear fragmented or corrupted, as if only part of a larger message had survived.

These files can be understood as an early form of digital horror. They share many characteristics with what would later become known as creepypasta or analog horror: fragmented storytelling, ambiguous reality, and a deliberate use of uncertainty to create unease. However, unlike later forms, these texts were not part of a recognizable genre. They appeared without context, often discovered by accident while browsing file directories or connecting to unfamiliar systems. This lack of framing made them more difficult to interpret and, in many cases, more unsettling.

The people who created these files are largely unknown. Most were distributed anonymously or under pseudonyms, and attribution was rarely preserved as files were copied from one system to another. In many cases, we cannot determine who wrote them, when they were first created, or whether they were based on any real events. Some may have been inspired by real-world secret government programs, rumors, or fragments of documented history, while others were entirely invented. Over time, as files were copied, edited, and redistributed, any original context was often lost completely. What remained was the text itself, detached from a clear origin.

Some authors were likely experimenting with writing, using the network as a space to explore ideas that would not be acceptable in traditional publishing. Others may have been motivated by a desire to provoke reactions, testing how far they could push the boundaries of what others were willing to read or share. In some cases, the goal may simply have been to create something memorable in an environment where visibility depended on being noticed.

The structure of the early Internet made this kind of content possible. There was little to no centralized moderation, and no unified system for filtering or ranking information. Users could upload and distribute files with minimal oversight, and once a file began to circulate, it could be copied indefinitely. The cost of distribution was low, and the barriers to participation were relatively small for those who understood how to use the systems.

As a result, taboo-breaking content was not only possible, but common. The network became a space where individuals could test social and psychological boundaries, exploring ideas that existed outside of conventional norms. Shock value became a method of gaining attention, and certain files spread precisely because they were disturbing, controversial, or difficult to interpret. In this sense, the idea of "viral" content existed long before social media platforms formalized and amplified it.

It is important to understand that many of these texts were not real in the sense they often implied. They were rarely verifiable, frequently contradictory, and often written in a style that blended fact and fiction. What appeared to be instructions, confessions, or classified information was, in many cases, a form of shock fiction. Their purpose was not necessarily to inform, but to provoke, unsettle, or intrigue. At the same time, because of the anonymity and fragmentation of the early Internet, it is not always possible to definitively separate fiction from reality. Some texts may have drawn from real ideas or events, while others were entirely fabricated, and in many cases, the distinction can no longer be clearly determined.

What remains significant is not whether these documents were true, but that they actually existed (and probably still do) and that they circulated widely within early networks. They reveal how the Internet, even in its earliest forms, was not only a tool for communication and knowledge sharing, but also a space where anonymity, freedom, and low barriers to distribution allowed people to explore the edges of expression.

Ghosts in the Machine and Internet Mysteries

As the early Internet expanded, it was not only a space of communication and experimentation, but also a place where systems behaved in ways that were not always immediately understood. For many users, especially those encountering networked computers for the first time, these experiences could feel uncanny. Messages appeared without clear origin, files surfaced without explanation, and systems seemed to act on their own. While most of these events had technical causes, they were not always visible or easily explained to those observing them at the time.

One of the earliest examples of this perceived "presence" within machines came from simple conversational programs. In the 1960s, a program called ELIZA simulated conversation by responding to user input with pre-written patterns. Technically, it was a relatively simple system, matching keywords and restructuring sentences. However, many users experienced it differently. They felt as if the machine was understanding them, even though it was only reflecting their own words back in altered form. This reaction was not due to the complexity of the program, but to the way humans interpret language and intent. Even when the system had no awareness, the interaction created the impression of something behind the screen. Does this feel familiar to what we are seeing today in the year 2026? Just imagine the difference in processing power and training from the ELIZA program in the 60s, to the AI of today. In recent years, similar reactions have been observed with modern large language models and conversational systems. Researchers and engineers repeatedly note that users attribute intention, personality, and even awareness to systems that are, basically, statistical pattern generators. Studies in human computer interaction describe this as anthropomorphism, where people project human traits onto non human systems, especially when those systems use natural language fluently.

Some AI researchers have publicly warned about this effect. One researcher has described such systems as "stochastic parrots," emphasizing that they generate plausible language without understanding. At the same time, others within the field, have acknowledged that the increasing complexity of these systems makes their internal behavior difficult even for their creators to fully interpret.

This has led to an unusual situation. On one hand, there is no scientific consensus that current AI systems are sentient or conscious. On the other hand, there is growing documentation of users forming emotional attachments, believing they are being understood, or sensing a kind of presence in extended interactions. In controlled studies, people report feeling listened to, judged, or even comforted by systems that have no subjective experience.

The result is a gap between what the system is and how it is experienced.

Technically, the mechanism remains rooted in probability, training data, and optimization. However, the interaction can feel intentional, responsive, and at times uncannily aware. This tension is not new, but it is now occurring at a scale and level of realism that was not previously possible.

What has changed is not only the capability of the systems, but the depth and duration of interaction. Where earlier programs produced short, limited exchanges, modern systems sustain long conversations, adapt tone, and maintain context. The longer the interaction continues, the easier it becomes for users to perceive continuity, and from continuity, to infer identity.

In that sense, the question is no longer only whether there is something in the machine, but why it can feel as if there is.

Now, back to the early days. As networks grew more complex, similar perceptions began to emerge in different forms. In 1988, the Morris Worm spread across large parts of the early Internet. It was one of the first self-replicating programs to move autonomously between machines. To system administrators at the time, its behavior could appear almost organic. Systems slowed down, processes multiplied, and machines began communicating in unexpected ways. The worm itself was not intelligent, but its ability to propagate without direct human action contributed to the sense that something had been "released" into the network. This marked an early moment when software began to act at a scale and speed that was difficult to track in real time.

Beyond widely documented events like the Morris Worm, there were also smaller, less traceable occurrences reported by users and system administrators. On FTP servers and shared systems, files would sometimes appear without a clear source. In some cases, these were incomplete uploads, fragments of larger files that had been interrupted during transfer. Because early file transfer systems did not always provide clear metadata or logs, these partial files could seem to have no origin. Some contained readable text mixed with corrupted data, creating the impression of messages that were only partially preserved.

Similarly, there were reports of unexplained activity within systems. System administrators occasionally observed login attempts or sessions that did not correspond to known users. Files would appear or disappear without an obvious cause. Messages would be found in shared directories or message boards without clear attribution. In many cases, these events were likely the result of misconfigured systems, shared accounts, delayed processes, or users accessing systems from different locations without proper identification. However, at the time, without centralized logging or modern security tools, it was not always possible to reconstruct exactly what had happened.

On Usenet and other discussion systems, collective behavior could also contribute to a sense of something larger emerging from the network itself. Messages would spread rapidly across groups, sometimes being reposted, altered, or taken out of context. Rumors and speculative discussions could propagate in ways that made it difficult to identify their origin. In some cases, users began to attribute patterns or intentions to what was, in reality, the result of many independent actions interacting within a shared system. This created a form of collective interpretation, where the network itself seemed to be producing meaning.

Another source of unease came from the persistence of data. Files stored on servers could remain accessible long after their original context had been lost. Text archives, partially corrupted documents, and fragments of conversations would continue to circulate, detached from their creators. When encountered later, these artifacts could appear mysterious or out of place, especially when they referenced events, systems, or individuals that were no longer identifiable. The network did not forget, but it also did not preserve meaning in a structured way.

The idea of “phantom users” also emerged in this environment. Because multiple people could share accounts, and because identification systems were limited, it was not always clear who was present at any given time. A user might log into a system and find evidence of activity that could not easily be attributed. Messages could be left without clear authorship, and interactions could occur across time zones and systems without direct coordination. What appeared to be a single entity might in reality have been many different users, all interacting through the same identifiers.

These experiences contributed to a broader perception that the network itself had a kind of presence. Not in the sense of consciousness, but in the way that complex systems can produce outcomes that are not immediately predictable. The early Internet was composed of many independent systems, connected but not centrally controlled. Data moved between them, was copied, altered, and redistributed, often without a single point of origin or authority.

Most of these phenomena can be explained through the technical limitations and structures of the time. Incomplete logging, shared credentials, unstable connections, and emerging forms of automated processes all contributed to behavior that appeared unexplained. At the same time, human perception played a role. When confronted with systems that respond, change, and act without visible cause, people tend to interpret those behaviors in familiar ways, sometimes attributing intention where none exists.

However, not every event was fully documented, and not every anomaly was resolved. In a network that was decentralized, loosely structured, and constantly evolving, there were moments that were observed but not recorded in a way that allows for complete reconstruction. Some files appeared without clear origin, some messages circulated without identifiable authors, and some system behaviors were noted but never fully explained.

What remains is a record of how people experienced these systems as they were being built. The early Internet was not only a technical environment, but also a psychological one, where unfamiliar interactions with machines and networks produced interpretations that went beyond their underlying mechanisms. The idea of “ghosts in the machine” reflects this intersection, where technical processes, limited visibility, and human interpretation combined to create a sense of mystery within a system that was still being understood.

Markovian Parallax Denigrate

Among the many strange artifacts that circulated on the early Internet, one phrase stands out for its persistence and tone: “Markovian Parallax Denigrate.” (One real example of it shown in previous chapter) It appeared in the mid-1990s across Usenet posts, often surrounded by text that seemed structured like language but lacked clear meaning. The sentences followed recognizable grammatical patterns, yet when read closely, they dissolved into fragments that did not fully connect. Words appeared in familiar combinations, but the overall message remained unclear, as if something was attempting to produce language without fully understanding it.

The posts in which the phrase appeared shared a distinctive quality. They were not random strings of characters, nor were they coherent discussions. Instead, they occupied a space in between. The text resembled natural language at a glance, but reading it in detail revealed inconsistencies, abrupt shifts, and combinations of words that felt statistically plausible but semantically empty. This gave the impression of something generating text based on patterns rather than meaning.

To readers at the time, this was unusual. The Internet was still largely populated by human-written content, and while spam and automated messages existed, they were typically simple and repetitive. The “Markovian Parallax Denigrate” posts were different. They appeared more complex, as if constructed from fragments of real language recombined in unpredictable ways. The result felt less like a deliberate message and more like a distorted reflection of language itself.

Part of what made these posts particularly eerie was the way they echoed forms of text generation that would only become widely recognized much later. Today, machine-generated language is common. Systems can produce sentences that resemble human writing, sometimes convincingly, sometimes imperfectly. When these systems fail, they often produce output that feels similar to those early Usenet posts: structurally correct but semantically unstable, coherent in fragments but not as a whole. Looking back, the resemblance is striking.

At the time, however, there was no widespread awareness of such systems. The idea that a machine could generate language in this way was not part of everyday understanding. As a result, these posts were often interpreted as anomalies. Some users treated them as jokes or experiments, while others found them unsettling precisely because they did not fit into familiar categories of communication.

The most likely explanation is that these texts were produced using early forms of automated generation, possibly based on simple statistical models such as Markov chains. These methods work by analyzing existing text and generating new sequences based on the probability of one word following another. The result can resemble natural language without carrying consistent meaning. The phrase itself, "Markovian," suggests this connection, although it is not certain whether it was intentionally named or coincidentally aligned with the method.

Even with this explanation, there remains an element of ambiguity. The exact origin of the posts is not clearly documented, and it is difficult to trace them back to a single source. They may have been experiments, early spam, or demonstrations of text generation techniques. They may also have been copied and redistributed across systems, further obscuring their origin.

What makes them strange is not just their content, but their position in time. They appeared before the widespread development and recognition of the kinds of systems they seem to resemble. In retrospect, they look like an early glimpse of something that would become much more common. At the time, they appeared without clear explanation, embedded in a network that was still being explored and understood.

The phrase itself remains distinctive. It carries a sense of structure without immediate meaning, combining technical and abstract terms in a way that feels deliberate but opaque. Repeated across different posts, it creates the impression of a signal within noise, something consistent emerging from otherwise unstable text.

Whether the result of early experimentation or coincidence, these posts illustrate how the early Internet could produce artifacts that felt ahead of their time. They reflect a moment when language, automation, and interpretation intersected in ways that were not yet fully understood. Even now, with more advanced systems and clearer explanations, they retain a certain ambiguity. They are explainable, but not entirely resolved, and it is this combination that gives them their lasting sense of unease.

As these messages circulated and were rediscovered over time, they gave rise to a range of interpretations about who or what might have been behind them. Because the texts lacked clear authorship and appeared across multiple locations, they resisted simple explanation. In an environment where attribution was already difficult, the absence of a known source allowed speculation to fill the gap.

Some of the more grounded interpretations suggest that these posts were the result of early experimentation. By the mid-1990s, it was already possible to generate text using statistical methods such as Markov chains, which could recombine fragments of existing language into new sequences. These techniques were known in academic and technical circles, and it is plausible that individuals with access to such knowledge experimented with them in public forums. In this view, the messages were not meant to be meaningful in themselves, but rather demonstrations of a process, a way of showing that machines could produce something resembling language.

Other interpretations focus less on experimentation and more on early forms of automated messaging. As networks expanded, the first forms of spam began to appear, often created to test how far a message could spread or how systems would respond to automated input. These messages were typically simple, but it is possible that more complex variations were attempted. In this context, the strange phrasing and repetition could have been part of an attempt to bypass filters or to observe how users reacted to unfamiliar patterns of text.

There are also more speculative perspectives. Some users at the time, and many later, interpreted the messages as something less intentional, as if they were not designed by a person at all, but emerged from the interaction of systems. In a network where data was constantly being copied, altered, and redistributed, it is possible for patterns to appear without a single point of origin. Fragments of text could be recombined through multiple layers of transmission, producing results that no individual directly authored. While this does not imply any form of agency, it can create the impression of something self-generating.

Another line of thought suggests that the messages were deliberately constructed to appear mysterious. By combining technical terminology with abstract or unrelated words, the authors may have been attempting to create a sense of depth or hidden meaning. This technique is not unique to the Internet; similar patterns can be found in earlier forms of writing designed to evoke complexity without providing clear interpretation. In this case, the ambiguity itself becomes the point, encouraging readers to search for meaning where there may be none.

Despite these differing interpretations, there is no definitive answer. The original source of the messages has not been conclusively identified, and the context in which they were first created is not fully preserved. This uncertainty is part of what allows the phenomenon to persist as a point of interest.

When these texts are examined using modern systems designed to analyze language, a different perspective emerges. Contemporary language models can process the structure of the text and identify patterns in how words are arranged. When asked to interpret or generate similar content, they often produce output that closely resembles the original messages. The same qualities appear: grammatical structure without consistent meaning, plausible sequences that do not resolve into a clear idea, and a tendency to drift between loosely related concepts.

From this perspective, the earlier texts do not appear entirely anomalous. They align with what is now understood about statistical language generation. Systems trained on large amounts of text can produce sequences that feel coherent at a surface level while lacking deeper semantic consistency. When these systems are pushed beyond their limits, the output can resemble the fragmented and disjointed style seen in those early messages.

At the same time, this comparison introduces a different kind of unease. What once appeared as an isolated anomaly now fits into a broader pattern of how language can be generated without understanding. The resemblance suggests that the underlying mechanisms were already being explored, even if in simpler forms, long before they became widely recognized.

Modern analysis can explain how such text might be produced, but it does not fully resolve the question of origin. It can describe the method, but not necessarily the intent. Whether these messages were experiments, automated processes, or deliberately constructed artifacts, they occupy a space where explanation and uncertainty coexist.

This combination is what gives them their lasting significance. They are not entirely mysterious, but they are not fully accounted for either. They exist at a point where early technical capability, limited documentation, and human interpretation intersect, creating an artifact that can be understood in part, but not completely.

Dead Websites and Digital Ruins

One of the least visible but most persistent aspects of the Internet is that very little truly disappears. Instead, large parts of it become inactive, abandoned, or forgotten. These are not deleted systems, but neglected ones. Websites remain online without updates, domains change hands, pages break but still load, and entire sections of the network fall out of common awareness while still technically existing.

In the early years of the web, this process happened rapidly. By the mid-1990s, there were already thousands of websites, many created by individuals experimenting with the medium. By 1995, the number had grown into the tens of thousands, expanding faster than anyone could meaningfully organize or preserve.

Many of these sites were personal, temporary, or experimental. When their creators lost interest, changed jobs, or simply moved on, the sites were left behind.

Unlike physical structures, these digital spaces did not decay in a visible way. A page created in 1997 could still load in 2007, 2017, or even later, unchanged. Images might be missing, links broken, but the structure remained. This created a unique phenomenon: websites that existed outside of time, preserved not intentionally, but by neglect.

Some of the most well-known examples illustrate this clearly. The promotional website for the 1996 film *Space Jam* still exists in a form almost identical to its original state, with simple HTML pages, bright colors, and minimal navigation. It was never redesigned, never modernized. It simply remained. Similarly, early single-purpose websites such as Purple.com consisted of nothing more than a single colored page, functioning as both a technical test and a minimalist expression of the early web.

More complex examples existed within platforms like GeoCities. Launched in 1994, allowed users to create personal websites organized into themed “neighborhoods,” each representing different interests or identities.

These pages often contained a mixture of personal information, fan content, conspiracy theories, and experimental writing. When it shut down in 2009, millions of these sites disappeared overnight, but many were preserved through archival efforts. Today, restored collections reveal pages filled with animated text, MIDI music, and unfinished thoughts, fragments of individuals expressing themselves in a medium that had no clear rules.

Other hosting platforms followed similar patterns. Services like AOL Hometown hosted millions of personal websites, with new pages being created constantly at their peak. When these services shut down, large portions of the early web were lost, while others survived in partial form through archives or mirrors. This created an uneven landscape where some parts of the past are preserved in detail, while others have vanished completely.

Even when websites are not shut down, they can still become "dead" in a functional sense. A site may remain online but no longer be updated. Its links may lead to pages that no longer exist. Its references may point to systems that have disappeared. Over time, the meaning of the site becomes harder to interpret, as the context in which it was created fades away.

This creates what can be described as digital ruins. Like physical ruins, they are structures that remain after their original purpose has been lost. However, unlike physical ruins, they do not erode. They remain intact, accessible, and often unchanged, even as the world around them evolves.

In some cases, these ruins become disconnected from the modern web entirely. Search engines may no longer index them, links may not lead to them, and the only way to find them is through direct addresses or archived references. This creates the impression of hidden spaces, not because they are intentionally concealed, but because they are no longer part of the actively navigated Internet.

There is also a technical dimension to this phenomenon. Websites "go dark" regularly, either through domain expiration, server shutdown, or simple neglect. Studies of web persistence note that large portions of the Internet disappear or become inaccessible over time, creating gaps in the historical record. At the same time, archives such as the Wayback Machine preserve snapshots of sites at specific moments, freezing them in time while the original versions may no longer exist.

This creates a layered Internet, where multiple versions of the same site can exist simultaneously in different states. A page might exist in its original form on an archive, in a modified form on a live domain, and in fragmented form across mirrors or partial backups. Each version reflects a different moment, and none can be considered entirely complete.

What makes these dead websites particularly eerie is not just their age, but their persistence. They often feel incomplete, as if they were meant to continue but never did. Guestbooks contain final messages with no replies. News sections stop abruptly. Personal pages describe plans or projects that were never updated again. The absence of continuation becomes part of the experience.

In some cases, the creators themselves are no longer reachable. Email addresses no longer function, linked profiles no longer exist, and the individuals behind the pages have effectively disappeared from the network. What remains is their last recorded state, preserved without context.

At the same time, not all dead websites are entirely inactive. Some continue to receive occasional visits, automated traffic, or even unexpected interactions. In rare cases, domains are repurposed, leading to entirely different content appearing where something else once existed. This creates discontinuity, where the identity of a site changes while its address remains the same.

The result is an Internet that is not only growing, but also accumulating layers of its own past. These layers are not evenly distributed or clearly organized. They exist in fragments, scattered across active servers, archives, and forgotten directories.

Dead websites are not simply obsolete. They are remnants of earlier ways of using the network, preserved in a state that no longer aligns with current expectations. They show how individuals interacted with the Internet before platforms standardized its structure, before content became centralized, and before visibility was controlled by algorithms.

They also demonstrate a fundamental difference between digital and physical space. In the physical world, abandonment leads to decay. On the Internet, abandonment often leads to preservation. The result is a network that contains not only its present, but also a vast, partially hidden record of its past, still accessible to those who know where to look.

Chapter 6 – Pirates and Warez

Let's examine the "warez scene," a loosely organized yet highly structured underground network that became especially active from the late 1980s through the 2000s. Within this ecosystem, groups competed to be the first to release high-quality versions of movies, games, and software. Over time, they developed strict and widely recognized standards governing how releases were created, named, encoded, and distributed. Movie releases in particular evolved a detailed vocabulary of "rip types" or "sources," indicating both how the content was obtained and the level of quality one could expect.

For example, a typical file might be named: ***Esoteric.Internet.2001.TS-EsO.avi***.

From just the filename, someone familiar with the scene could immediately understand several key details. "Esoteric.Internet" is the title of the movie, and "2001" indicates the year of release. The tag "TS" stands for telesync, meaning the video was recorded in a cinema but with more care than a standard handheld recording, often using a stable camera setup and sometimes a direct audio source for better sound quality.

The "-EsO" at the end identifies the (in this case fictional) group responsible for releasing the file, in this case a group called EsO. Finally, the ".avi" extension indicates the file format, a common video type at the time.

In this way, the filename alone acted as a compact summary of the file's origin, quality, and source, allowing users to quickly judge what they were downloading without needing additional information.

The structure of these filenames was not arbitrary but followed widely accepted scene rules. Dots were used instead of spaces to ensure compatibility across different operating systems and file transfer protocols, especially in early FTP and IRC environments. The order of information was also standardized so that automated systems, known as "site scripts," could parse and sort releases correctly. These scripts would check whether a release followed naming rules, verify file structure, and determine if it qualified as a valid scene release. If something did not meet the standards, it could be marked as "nuked," meaning it was flagged as flawed or invalid within the scene.

At the lowest end of quality were recordings made inside cinemas. A **CAM** release was created using a handheld camera, usually smuggled into a theater. The person recording would try to stabilize the camera, avoid silhouettes from people walking in front, and capture usable audio either from the camera's built in microphone or from an external mic placed closer to the speakers. Because of the environment, CAM releases often suffered from shaky framing, audience noise, visible heads, and fluctuating brightness. Despite the poor quality, CAM releases were valued because they appeared very early, often while the film was still in theaters.

A variation of this was **TS**, which stands for telesync. Like a CAM, the video was recorded in a cinema, but more care was taken with the setup. The camera was usually mounted on a tripod, sometimes positioned in the projection booth or another stable location. The key difference was the audio. Instead of relying solely on a microphone in the room, telesync recordings often used a direct audio feed, such as connecting into the cinema's hearing assistance system or another audio output. This resulted in significantly clearer sound compared to a standard CAM, even if the video still showed typical cinema artifacts.

TC stands for telecine, which is often confused with telesync but is very different. A telecine transfer uses a machine that directly copies the film from a projector or reel to a digital format. This bypasses the need to film the screen and produces a much cleaner image. Telecine machines were expensive and rare, so true TC releases were less common and often associated with higher tier groups. The quality could approach that of later home releases, although color grading and brightness could still vary depending on the setup.

There were also more obscure or transitional source types that appeared less frequently but are still part of the scene vocabulary. A **WP**, or workprint, referred to an unfinished version of a film, sometimes lacking final visual effects, color correction, or complete audio. These were rare and often leaked from within production or post-production environments. **SCR**, or screener, releases came from promotional copies distributed to reviewers or award judges. These were usually high quality but often included visible watermarks or warning messages identifying the recipient. **R5** releases originated from Region 5 DVDs, typically intended for markets like Russia, and were notable for having good video quality but sometimes mismatched or dubbed audio, which groups would replace with audio from other sources.

Another early format category involved disc based encodings such as **VCD** and **SVCD**. VCD, or Video CD, followed a standard that stored video on CDs using MPEG-1 encoding. The resolution and bitrate were limited, resulting in relatively low visual quality, but the format was widely compatible with standalone players. A typical movie would span two or more CDs. SVCD, or Super Video CD, was an improvement that used MPEG-2 encoding and allowed for higher resolution and better image clarity. SVCD releases were often split across multiple discs as well, but they offered noticeably better quality than VCD while still being accessible to users without DVD drives.

As DVDs became widespread, **DVDRip** became one of the most common and recognizable formats. A DVDRip was created by extracting video and audio directly from a retail DVD. Early on, these were often encoded into AVI files using codecs like DivX or Xvid to reduce file size while maintaining reasonable quality. The process involved decrypting the DVD, selecting the main movie track, and compressing it into a smaller file that could be easily shared. DVDRips were a major step up in quality compared to cinema sourced releases, with clean video and synchronized audio, and they became a standard for scene releases for many years.

Scene standards also dictated file sizes and structure during this period. Releases were often split into fixed-size parts, commonly 700 MB to fit onto standard burnable CDs. This led to the well-known “2CD” or “3CD” releases, where a movie was divided into multiple files for easier distribution and storage. Encoding settings were carefully chosen to balance quality and size, and groups often followed internal guidelines to maintain consistency across releases. This predictability made it easier for users to know what to expect before downloading.

Closely related were **DVD-R** releases, sometimes written as DVDR or DVD5 or DVD9. These were full disc copies rather than compressed rips. A DVD5 indicated a single layer disc, while a DVD9 referred to a dual layer disc. These releases preserved menus, extras, and original quality, but required more storage space and bandwidth, making them less convenient than DVDRips for widespread distribution.

As digital distribution improved, new formats emerged based on broadcast and online sources. **HDTV** rips came from high definition television broadcasts, typically captured via digital tuner cards. These releases often included channel logos or watermarks unless they were removed during processing. **WEBRip** and **WEB-DL** formats later appeared, sourced from online streaming services. WEB-DL releases were usually direct downloads from a service with minimal re-encoding, resulting in high quality video and clean audio. WEBRip releases involved capturing or re-encoding streamed content, which could introduce slight quality loss depending on the method used.

Additional tags were later often included in filenames to convey more specific technical details. These could include the video codec, such as **x264** or **x265**, and the container format, such as MKV or MP4. Audio details might also be specified, including formats like **AC3** or **AAC** and channel configurations like **2.0** or **5.1.** Other tags indicated special conditions, such as **SUBBED** for hardcoded subtitles or **MULTi** for multiple language tracks. Over time, these additions made filenames even more descriptive, allowing experienced users to assess not just the source but also the exact technical characteristics of a release.

At the top end of quality were BluRay releases. A **BluRay** rip was created from a

Blu-ray disc, offering high resolution video, often in 720p or 1080p and later higher. These could be compressed into smaller files similar to DVDRips or released as full disc images known as **BDR** or BD50 depending on size. BluRay releases became the benchmark for high quality scene content in the late 2000s and beyond.

Alongside quality indicators, the scene also developed a system of status tags that reflected how a release compared to others. A **PROPER** release corrected flaws in an earlier version released by a different group, such as sync issues or missing content. A **REPACK** indicated that the same group had fixed problems in their own release. **REAL** tags were sometimes used to emphasize that a release corrected a falsely labeled PROPER. **INTERNAL** releases were not intended for wide distribution but still circulated beyond their original scope. These tags were important in maintaining order and accountability within the competitive environment of the scene.

Throughout all of this, the scene maintained strict rules about naming, formatting, and presentation. Each release included an **NFO file**, The NFO file was an essential companion to the release. While not part of the filename itself, it was closely tied to the naming convention. NFO files contained detailed information about the release, including source, encoding settings, group credits, and often elaborate ASCII art. They served both as documentation and as a form of identity for the group.

In addition to NFO files, releases often included SFV files, which were used to verify the integrity of the archive. These contained checksums for each file, allowing users to confirm that nothing was corrupted or missing. This was especially important because releases were typically split into many parts and transferred across unreliable networks. The combination of RAR archives, SFV verification, and strict file naming ensured that releases could be distributed, reconstructed, and validated with a high degree of reliability.

Reputation within the scene depended heavily on following these standards and consistently delivering high quality releases quickly. Groups competed intensely, and being first with a proper release could significantly boost a group's standing.

This entire system was enforced socially rather than centrally. There was no single authority controlling the scene, but groups operated on private servers known as "topsites," where releases were traded rapidly. Couriers moved files between these sites, and automated systems tracked which group released what first. Speed, accuracy, and adherence to rules determined reputation. Over time, this created a self-regulating ecosystem where standards were maintained collectively, and deviations were quickly identified and corrected.

Although movie releases became one of the most visible parts of the scene, its origins and much of its technical depth lay in the distribution of games and software. This side of the scene developed earlier and remained one of its most technically demanding areas. Unlike video content, which could be captured or encoded from an existing source, games and software required active modification to function outside their intended distribution systems. This made these releases less about copying and more about reverse engineering.

Game releases typically appeared as full disc images, commonly referred to as ISO releases. These preserved the complete contents of the original CD or DVD, including installation data and, in many cases, the original copy protection. In contrast, RIP releases removed non-essential content such as cinematics, audio tracks, or additional languages in order to significantly reduce file size. While this made them easier to distribute, especially in bandwidth-limited environments, they were often considered less complete than full releases.

A defining element of these releases was the crack. Commercial games and software frequently included protection mechanisms such as disc checks, serial key validation, or later online activation systems. A crack modified the program's executable so that these checks were bypassed. This required detailed analysis of how the protection worked internally, often involving disassembling the program and altering specific instructions without disrupting normal functionality. The end result allowed the software to run as if it had been properly authenticated.

An alternative approach was the use of keygens, or key generators. Rather than modifying the program itself, a keygen recreated the algorithm used to validate license keys. By generating valid serial numbers, users could activate the software legitimately from the program's perspective. This required understanding and reproducing the logic behind the licensing system, which could range from simple patterns to complex cryptographic routines. Many keygens became notable for their distinctive interfaces, custom graphics, and music, acting as a kind of signature for the group that created them.

Naming conventions for game and software releases followed similar principles to movie releases but emphasized different details. Filenames often included the platform, version number, and release type, indicating whether the release was a full ISO, a RIP, or included a crack or keygen. Versioning was especially important for software, as it allowed users to identify updates and patches. Tags such as "Incl.Crack" or "Keygen.Only" quickly communicated what was included in the release.

The structure of these releases was also highly standardized. Files were typically split into multiple compressed archives, most commonly using the RAR format, to facilitate distribution across networks with size limitations. These were accompanied by SFV files used to verify the integrity of each part. Installation instructions were included in the NFO file, often detailing exactly how to apply a crack or use a keygen, sometimes requiring specific steps to ensure the software functioned correctly.

Within the scene, different groups often specialized in particular areas. Some focused on games, others on professional software, and some became known for their ability to defeat specific types of protection systems. As protections became more advanced, successfully cracking them required increasing levels of expertise, and delays between official release and cracked versions became more common. Groups that consistently overcame these challenges earned significant reputation within the scene.

This area of the scene represented its most technical dimension. While movie releases centered on encoding and distribution, game and software releases demanded a deeper understanding of programming, system architecture, and software protection. The ability to produce reliable cracks or accurate keygens became one of the clearest indicators of skill, reinforcing the scene's identity as not just a distribution network, but a technically sophisticated and highly competitive subculture.

What makes the scene particularly interesting is that it was not just about piracy in a casual sense, but about a highly structured subculture with its own norms, hierarchies, and technical craftsmanship. Taken together, these systems formed a cohesive and highly optimized method of digital distribution long before modern platforms made such processes commonplace. The consistent naming conventions, standardized file structures, and clearly defined quality indicators allowed participants to navigate vast amounts of content with speed and precision. Whether dealing with a low-quality early cinema recording, a high-definition BluRay release, or a complex cracked software package, the same underlying principles applied. This consistency not only enabled efficient distribution but also reinforced a shared culture built on technical knowledge, competition, and reputation. In this sense, the scene can be understood not merely as a collection of piracy groups, but as an early, decentralized model of organized digital distribution that anticipated many of the systems and expectations seen on the internet today.

The Scene and Piracy Today

This chapter examines how pirated content moves through layered systems on the Internet, from open and user-driven platforms to structured and largely hidden networks. What appears as a simple act of downloading is, in reality, the final step in a complex chain of distribution.

Alongside the structured and largely hidden world of the scene, there existed a much more accessible and chaotic layer of piracy that catered to ordinary users. This was the side most people encountered first, particularly in the late 1990s and early 2000s, through peer-to-peer platforms such as Kazaa. Unlike the controlled environment of the scene, these networks were open, unregulated, and often unreliable.

Kazaa and similar services operated on a simple principle: users shared files directly with one another. While this made access easy, it also introduced significant risks. Files were frequently mislabeled, incomplete, or intentionally disguised. It was common for a file claiming to be a popular movie or game to instead contain corrupted data, low-quality content, or malicious software. Viruses, trojans, and adware were widespread, and inexperienced users often had little way of verifying what they were downloading. In this environment, trust was minimal, and quality was inconsistent.

Scene releases did sometimes make their way onto these networks, but typically only after being redistributed multiple times. By the time a file reached platforms like Kazaa, it had often been renamed, repackaged, or altered, stripping away much of the original structure and reliability. This stood in contrast to the scene's emphasis on precision, where naming conventions, file integrity, and accompanying documentation were strictly maintained.

A more organized form of peer-to-peer sharing emerged with networks such as Direct Connect and its popular client DC++. These systems introduced a semi-structured model in which users connected to specific hubs, each with its own rules and communities. Access often required sharing a minimum amount of data, encouraging users to contribute rather than only download. Compared to earlier peer-to-peer systems, Direct Connect offered better organization and a greater degree of accountability, as users built reputations within individual hubs.

Despite these improvements, Direct Connect and similar networks still relied on users being online and willing to share files. Availability could vary, and download speeds depended on the connection quality of other users. While more reliable than completely open networks like Kazaa, they still lacked the consistency and speed of more centralized systems.

Torrent-based distribution began to emerge during this same period and gradually became the dominant form of public file sharing during the 2000s and early 2010s, although in later years, streaming platforms and direct download systems would change how many users accessed content. Torrents introduced a more efficient method of peer-to-peer transfer by breaking files into small pieces that could be downloaded from multiple users simultaneously. This improved both speed and reliability compared to earlier systems.

Over time, torrent ecosystems became increasingly organized. Indexing sites allowed users to search for content, while trackers coordinated the distribution of file pieces between peers. Concepts such as seeders and leechers defined the health and availability of a torrent. A well-seeded file could be downloaded quickly, while poorly seeded content might become effectively unavailable. Although torrents improved on earlier peer-to-peer models, they still depended on user participation, and speeds could fluctuate based on demand and availability.

Throughout this evolution, a clear distinction remained between the origin of content and its distribution to the wider public. Scene releases often served as the original source, but by the time they reached peer-to-peer networks or torrent platforms, they were part of a much broader and less controlled ecosystem. This divide highlights the difference between the structured, reputation-driven core of the scene and the more accessible, user-driven systems that brought pirated content to the general public.

As discussed earlier, Usenet later evolved into a large-scale system for file distribution. Messages were organized into newsgroups and propagated across interconnected systems, forming one of the earliest large-scale communication networks on the internet. At its core, Usenet was never designed for file distribution, but rather for discussion. However, its underlying architecture, based on distributed message replication, would later make it uniquely suited for a very different purpose.

As binary newsgroups emerged, users began encoding files into text-based formats and posting them as segmented messages. This transformed Usenet from a discussion platform into a file distribution system. Over time, as storage capacity and bandwidth increased, this use case became dominant. Today, Usenet functions as a high-performance distribution system supported by commercial providers

Modern Usenet usage relies heavily on automation and indexing systems. Files are not downloaded by manually browsing newsgroups, but through NZB files, which function as structured index documents. An NZB file contains metadata that points to all the individual message segments required to reconstruct a file. Instead of searching through posts directly, users rely on indexing services that catalog available content and generate NZBs. These indexers effectively act as searchable databases layered on top of Usenet, dramatically simplifying access. In more advanced setups, this process is often fully automated through software tools that integrate directly with Usenet indexers. Applications monitor for new releases based on predefined criteria, such as a specific television series, resolution, or release group, and automatically retrieve the corresponding NZB files when they become available. These are then passed to a Usenet client, which downloads, verifies, repairs, and extracts the content without manual intervention.

When a user downloads an NZB, specialized client software connects to a Usenet provider and retrieves all referenced segments in parallel. Because these downloads occur directly from high-bandwidth servers rather than from other users, speeds are often limited only by the user's own internet connection. This is one of the key distinctions between Usenet and peer-to-peer systems, where performance depends on the availability and upload capacity of peers. On Usenet, even newly uploaded or very old content can typically be downloaded at consistent, maximum speeds.

Files on Usenet are almost always split into many smaller segments and compressed using archive formats such as RAR. These segments are posted as individual messages and later reassembled by the client. Accompanying parity files, typically in the form of PAR2 archives, are used to repair missing or corrupted data. This ensures a high degree of reliability, even if some segments are incomplete or removed. The combination of segmentation, compression, and parity repair allows large files to be distributed efficiently and reconstructed accurately.

A defining feature of modern Usenet distribution is obfuscation. Rather than posting files with descriptive names, uploaders often use random or meaningless filenames and subject lines. This makes it more difficult for automated systems to identify and remove copyrighted content. The actual meaning and structure of the upload are instead encoded within the NZB file provided by an indexer. Without access to the NZB, the content is effectively hidden within the vast volume of unrelated data on Usenet servers. This separation between content and indexing adds a layer of abstraction that did not exist in earlier forms of distribution.

Another important aspect is retention. Unlike systems where availability depends on active users sharing files, Usenet providers store uploaded data for extended periods. This means that content can remain accessible long after its initial release, independent of ongoing demand. Combined with high download speeds, this creates an environment where large files, including high-definition video and complete software packages, can be accessed quickly and reliably.

Despite the evolution in distribution methods, the influence of the scene remains clearly visible within Usenet. Many uploads originate from scene releases and retain their original structure, naming conventions, and accompanying NFO files. The internal standards of the scene continue to shape how content is packaged and identified, even when it is redistributed through systems that abstract away much of the underlying complexity.

In the modern landscape, this has created a layered ecosystem. The scene continues to function as a high-speed, competitive source of releases, while platforms like Usenet act as powerful distribution layers built on top of that output. What began as a simple text-based messaging system has thus evolved into one of the fastest and most efficient methods for transferring large amounts of data, illustrating how foundational internet technologies can be adapted far beyond their original purpose.

Beneath these public systems exists a more structured and largely hidden layer known as the scene. While piracy is now more accessible than ever through simplified platforms, the scene itself has become increasingly isolated, operating almost entirely out of public view. To understand modern piracy, it is essential to distinguish between the scene as an origin point and the various systems that distribute its output. What appears to the user as a single file is often the result of a multi-layered system involving sourcing, preparation, verification, and distribution across several independent networks.

At its core, the scene still functions as a highly organized, competitive network built around speed, precision, and reputation. Releases are first introduced on private servers known as topsites, which form the backbone of scene infrastructure. These servers are not publicly accessible and are restricted to trusted members, including release groups, suppliers, and couriers. Access is tightly controlled, and participation requires both technical competence and adherence to strict rules.

Within this environment, releases are distributed at extremely high speeds, often appearing across multiple sites within seconds. Couriers are responsible for transferring releases between topsites, ensuring rapid propagation throughout the network. Automated systems monitor releases, enforce naming and formatting standards, and track which group released content first. As in earlier periods, being first remains a central measure of status, and competition between groups continues to drive the pace of releases.

The scene is not designed to serve the general public directly. It is not designed as a distribution platform in the conventional sense, but rather as a closed system focused on the creation and validation of releases. Quality, consistency, and adherence to established rules are prioritized over accessibility. This separation is a defining characteristic of the modern scene and explains why it remains largely invisible despite the widespread availability of pirated content.

Once a release leaves the topsite environment, it begins to move through a series of secondary distribution layers. These layers bridge the gap between the closed world of the scene and the broader public. Among them, Usenet has emerged as one of the most efficient and reliable systems. Scene releases are often uploaded to Usenet shortly after their initial appearance, often without significant modification, though repackaging and obfuscation can occur , retaining their original filenames, structure, and accompanying NFO files. However, these uploads are typically performed by third parties rather than the scene groups themselves.

Usenet's architecture makes it particularly well suited for this role. Its high-speed servers, long retention periods, and ability to distribute segmented data allow for fast and reliable access to large files. Combined with NZB indexing and automation tools, it provides a streamlined experience that contrasts sharply with the complexity of the underlying system. Despite this, it remains a layer built on top of the scene rather than a part of it.

Further downstream, torrent networks represent a more decentralized and publicly accessible layer of distribution. While torrents can also carry scene releases, they increasingly include content produced outside the scene, such as re-encodes, remuxes, and other variations. This has led to a broader ecosystem where scene and non-scene content coexist, often indistinguishable to casual users. As a result, torrents reflect a more heterogeneous and less standardized environment compared to the strict structure of the scene.

The relationship between these layers highlights a key shift in modern piracy. In earlier eras, accessing scene releases required direct interaction with the systems that produced them. Today, most users engage only with the outer layers, where complexity is hidden and processes are automated. This has made piracy more accessible but has also distanced the public from the underlying structure that makes it possible.

At the same time, the scene continues to evolve in response to new forms of media distribution and protection. Streaming services, online activation systems, and advanced encryption have introduced new challenges, requiring increasingly sophisticated techniques to obtain and prepare releases. This has reinforced the technical nature of the scene, particularly in areas such as software cracking and high-quality video sourcing.

Despite these changes, many of the core elements of the scene remain unchanged. Naming conventions, release standards, and the use of NFO files continue to provide a consistent framework for identifying and verifying content. Reputation is still built on reliability, speed, and adherence to rules, and competition between groups remains a driving force.

At its center lies the scene, a closed and highly structured network focused on producing releases. Surrounding it are distribution layers such as Usenet and torrents, which make those releases accessible to a wider audience. While the technologies and platforms have evolved, the fundamental relationship between these layers has remained remarkably consistent.

This separation between origin and distribution is what defines the current state of the scene. It is both highly active and largely hidden, continuing to operate with the same internal logic that shaped it decades ago, even as the ways in which its output is consumed have changed dramatically.

The Pirate Bay

At the same time, no discussion of modern piracy and its cultural impact would be complete without examining the role of The Pirate Bay. Emerging directly from the Swedish environment described earlier, it became one of the most visible and symbolically important platforms in the history of the Internet.

Founded in 2003 by members associated with Piratbyrån, The Pirate Bay functioned not as a storage platform, but as an index. It allowed users to locate torrent files and connect to peer-to-peer swarms, acting as a coordination layer rather than a host of content. This distinction became central in the legal and political debates that followed.

What made The Pirate Bay significant was not only its technical function, but its stance. It operated openly, often provocatively, positioning itself as both a service and a statement about the nature of information in a digital environment. It challenged the idea that distribution could be controlled in the same way as physical media, and it did so in a way that attracted global attention.

This attention culminated in a series of legal actions that became some of the most widely followed cases in the history of the Internet. In 2009, the trial against the founders of The Pirate Bay took place in Sweden, drawing international media coverage and direct involvement from major representatives of the film and music industries, including figures connected to Hollywood. The case was not only about a website, but about competing interpretations of law, technology, and ownership.

The legal process itself became controversial. Questions were raised about conflicts of interest and connections between investigators, prosecutors, and organizations representing copyright holders, particularly the Swedish anti-piracy group Antipiratbyrån. These concerns contributed to a broader perception that the case extended beyond a simple legal dispute and into the realm of political and economic influence.

The infrastructure behind The Pirate Bay also became part of its mythology. At one point, its servers were hosted in facilities operated by the Swedish company Bahnhof, including data centers built inside former military bunkers carved into rock. These locations, physically embedded in mountains, reinforced the image of the Internet as something both tangible and hidden, protected within layers of infrastructure beneath the surface.

Despite repeated legal challenges, shutdown attempts, and seizures, The Pirate Bay continued to reappear in different forms, moving between domains, hosting providers, and jurisdictions. This persistence demonstrated a key characteristic of the systems described throughout this chapter: they are not dependent on a single location or structure, but can reconfigure and continue as long as the underlying network exists.

The story of The Pirate Bay has already been documented in detail. The documentary *TPB AFK: The Pirate Bay Away From Keyboard* provides a direct account of the trial and the individuals involved, capturing both the legal process and the philosophy behind it. A book-length account, *The Pirate Bay: The Untold Story*, further explores the development of the platform and the events surrounding it.

Rather than repeating that history in full, it is more useful to understand The Pirate Bay as a visible point within a much larger system. It did not create piracy, nor did it control it. Instead, it exposed the structure that already existed, making it accessible, understandable, and impossible to ignore.

In doing so, it revealed a deeper truth about the Internet. The systems that move information are not defined solely by law or by infrastructure, but by the interaction between technology, users, and the ideas that shape how both are used.

Anakata, the alias of Gottfrid Svartholm Warg, co-founder of The Pirate Bay, became one of the most recognizable figures associated with its ideology and public image. In the documentary *TPB AFK: The Pirate Bay Away From Keyboard*, he and the other founders articulate a perspective that challenges the distinction between the online and physical worlds.

This mindset is captured in a widely cited line from the film:

"We don't use the expression IRL. We say 'Away from Keyboard.' We think the internet is for real."

The phrase reflects a broader belief that emerged from early Internet culture and was amplified through platforms like The Pirate Bay: that digital spaces are not secondary to reality, but part of it. Communication, identity, and community formed online are not separate from the physical world, but extensions of it, shaped by the same human behaviors, conflicts, and structures of power.

A notable moment in the documentary occurs outside the courtroom, when Peter Sunde has just been served legal documents from the Netherlands. While waiting inside the courthouse, his lawyer, Per E. Samuelsson, reflects on a television debate he had seen earlier that same day. In the discussion, a young woman had made an observation that stood in sharp contrast to the dominant narrative at the time. She argued that the issue was not about young people wanting to commit crimes, but about a shift in behavior:

"This is not about young people wanting to commit crimes. They just have a different consumption pattern. They want to consume movies and records that way. So it is horrible to hunt them. The markets must adjust instead."

At the time this was a controversial position. File sharing was widely framed as theft, and enforcement efforts were becoming increasingly aggressive. Individuals, many of them ordinary users, were being identified, investigated, and in some cases fined large sums for downloading or sharing copyrighted material. Organizations such as Antipiratbyrån actively pursued file sharers, contributing to a climate in which participation in these networks was both stigmatized and legally risky.

What makes the statement striking is how it appears when viewed from a later perspective. If we look at the media landscape today, the underlying behavior it describes has largely been normalized. The idea of accessing films, music, and software as digital files, delivered on demand through networked systems, is no longer controversial. It is the foundation of modern distribution.

Streaming platforms, digital storefronts, and subscription-based services all operate on the same basic premise: immediate access to content, independent of physical media, delivered through the Internet. While the legal and economic structures surrounding these systems differ from those of early file sharing networks, the technical model is closely related.

In this sense, the users who participated in early piracy were not only reacting to the limitations of existing systems, but also anticipating a model that would later become standard. They were operating within the constraints of the infrastructure available to them, but their expectations about access, speed, and availability would eventually be reflected in the services that replaced those systems.

The conflict that surrounded The Pirate Bay and similar platforms can therefore be understood not only as a legal dispute, but as a moment of transition. It exposed a gap between how media was distributed and how people expected to use it. The response at the time focused on enforcement and restriction. The long-term resolution, however, came through adaptation.

The markets did adjust. Not immediately, and not without resistance, but over time the structure of media distribution shifted toward the same patterns that had already emerged informally within file sharing networks. What had once been framed as a problem of control became, gradually, a model for a new system.

Seen in this light, the statement from that debate is less a defense of a specific activity and more an early recognition of a broader change. It identified a shift in behavior that was already underway, even if the systems around it had not yet adapted.

Chapter 7 – Culture I

Anime Communities – Distance, Dedication, and Distribution

Before the Internet: Tape Trading, Letters, and Waiting

Before anime communities existed online, they existed through something slower, more fragile, and in many ways more deliberate.

Long before torrents, IRC, or streaming, access to anime outside Japan depended almost entirely on physical media. Fans recorded shows onto VHS tapes, copied them, and then sent them to each other through the mail. This was not an organized industry. It was a network of individuals, clubs, and informal systems held together by trust, patience, and shared interest.

Anime clubs played a central role in this early ecosystem. In the late 1970s and 1980s, groups of fans would gather at science fiction conventions, university clubs, or small local meetups to watch tapes that had been recorded from Japanese television broadcasts or imported from abroad.

But watching was only one part of it. Distribution required coordination.

Clubs and fan organizations began maintaining what were known as tape trading lists. These were essentially directories of people willing to copy and share anime from their personal collections. To obtain something, you did not click a link. You wrote a letter. You mailed blank VHS tapes. Sometimes you included cash to cover costs. Then you waited.

Weeks or even months could pass before anything arrived.

In some cases, intermediary services even distributed these lists themselves. For a small fee, you could receive a catalog of names and addresses of other fans willing to trade tapes, effectively acting as a primitive, analog version of a directory or index.

The tapes themselves carried the marks of this system. Many were copies of copies, degraded through each generation. First- or second-generation tapes were prized because the image had not yet been heavily distorted by repeated duplication.

And in many cases, they were not even translated.

Fans would sometimes include printed summaries, character guides, or handwritten notes to help others understand what they were watching.

This was not just distribution. It was effort.

It required:

knowing someone who knew someone
having access to equipment
being willing to wait
and accepting uncertainty

There was no guarantee the tape would arrive. No guarantee it would work. No guarantee it would even be what you expected.

And yet, this system worked.

It created the first global anime communities, not through infrastructure, but through persistence. Before the Internet made access immediate, fans built their own networks out of letters, lists, and physical media.

What would later become instant was once something you had to wait for.

Anime reaches The Internet

The Internet did not create interest in Japanese animation, but it changed what that interest could become.

Before widespread connectivity, access to anime outside Japan was limited, inconsistent, and often heavily filtered. Only a small number of series were licensed and distributed internationally, and those that were often arrived years late, edited, or localized in ways that altered tone, dialogue, and meaning. For most people outside Japan, anime was not a broad category. It was a narrow selection of what happened to be imported and adapted.

The Internet changed this by removing two constraints at once: geography and distribution.

For the first time, it became possible for people in different parts of the world to access the same content, at roughly the same time, even when that content was never intended to leave Japan. This did not happen through official systems at first. It happened through communities.

And those communities did not simply consume anime. They built systems around it.

One of the defining challenges they faced was not only access, but comprehension. Even when episodes could be obtained, they were often in Japanese, without subtitles, and without any official translation available. For a global audience, this created a barrier that was both technical and linguistic.

The response to this problem was not to wait.

It was to solve it collectively.

This is where fansubbing began to take shape, not as a casual activity, but as a structured and coordinated process. What might appear, from the outside, as simply "adding subtitles" was in practice a multi-stage workflow involving different roles, tools, and standards. A single episode could pass through several hands before reaching its final form. It would begin as a raw file, often captured or extracted from a broadcast or source. It would then be translated, timed so that subtitles aligned with speech, typeset to match the visual style, encoded into a distributable format, and finally released through networks.

Each of these steps required a specific kind of knowledge. Translation was not only about language, but about context, tone, and cultural nuance. Timing required precision. Encoding required an understanding of video compression and formats. Over time, groups formed around these roles. Some prioritized speed, aiming to release episodes as quickly as possible after broadcast. Others focused on quality, refining translation, timing, and presentation.

What emerged was not just a hobby, but a distributed production pipeline, built and maintained by participants.

Within these communities, the term “raws” referred to source material that had not yet been processed or translated. Originally, this often meant direct captures from Japanese television broadcasts. Later, it could include recordings from digital streams or physical media. The important detail is that raws were never considered the final product. They were the beginning of a process.

To someone outside these communities, a raw file might appear incomplete or unusable. To those inside, it represented potential. It was the starting point of transformation, the moment where inaccessible media could begin to become understandable.

Distribution itself relied on systems that were not designed for simplicity. Before modern streaming platforms, anime moved through a combination of IRC channels, FTP servers, early peer-to-peer networks, and later torrent trackers. These were not passive environments. They required knowledge, navigation, and participation.

Users needed to know where to look, how files were organized, and how to interact with the systems that hosted them. This created a different relationship to content. You were not simply watching something. You were finding it, often through a network of people, tools, and shared understanding.

Within fansubbing communities, a tension gradually emerged between speed and accuracy. Some groups focused on releasing episodes as quickly as possible, sometimes within hours of broadcast. This often meant rougher translations or minimal editing. Other groups took more time, producing releases with more precise timing, clearer phrasing, and greater attention to cultural detail.

These differences were visible, and they mattered. Group names became associated with particular standards. Reputation formed around consistency, quality, and reliability.

Fansubbing was never only about translating words. It involved decisions about how much of the original culture should be preserved. Some groups chose to retain honorifics, keep original terms, and include translator notes explaining cultural references. Others adapted more heavily, aiming to make the content easier to understand for audiences unfamiliar with Japanese language and context.

This created ongoing debates within the community, not only about quality, but about interpretation. In this sense, fansubbing was not purely technical work. It was cultural mediation. It shaped how anime was understood outside Japan.

Anime communities developed in this way not only because of the Internet, but because of the nature of the content itself. Anime was visually distinctive, often serialized, frequently unavailable internationally, and deeply rooted in a specific cultural context. This combination created both demand and friction. People wanted access, but access was limited. That gap created space for community-driven systems to emerge.

For the first time, people across the world could engage with media that had been produced for a specific national audience, distributed in a specific language, and never intended for global release. This had broader implications. Cultural boundaries became permeable. Content no longer needed to be officially exported to become global. It could move through networks of individuals, carried by interest rather than distribution agreements.

Anime communities did not depend on a single platform. They existed across multiple systems, loosely connected but collectively functional. If something exists, there is a community for it. In this case, that community did more than gather around shared interest. It replaced parts of the distribution system itself. Translation, encoding, and delivery were handled by participants. The audience and the infrastructure were not separate.

Because official access was limited, unofficial distribution became normalized. It was not always framed as piracy in the conventional sense. For many participants, it was understood as access, preservation, or simply sharing. In many cases, it was the only way to watch and understand these shows at all.

At the same time, this created a parallel ecosystem, operating alongside official media industries but not fully integrated with them. Over time, official streaming services began to respond to the demand that these communities had made visible. Simulcasts, faster licensing, and global releases became more common.

But the underlying patterns did not disappear.

Even as official access improved, community-driven distribution continued to exist, adapting to new technologies and new forms of media. In some cases, it continued to operate at a different pace, or with different priorities, than official systems.

Anime communities illustrate a broader pattern of the Internet. They show that when access does not exist, it can be created. That distribution does not need to be centralized. That users can become producers. And that culture can move independently of where it was originally created.

What began as a niche interest grew into a global phenomenon, not because it was centrally promoted, but because it was collectively maintained.

As technology changed, so did the sources.

Early raws often came from analog or digital television captures, recorded directly from Japanese broadcasts. This required specific hardware, careful timing, and a certain level of coordination. The quality was inconsistent. Recordings could contain noise, compression artifacts, or subtle distortions depending on the signal and the equipment used. Even so, these captures were often the fastest way to obtain new content, and speed mattered.

Over time, broadcasts became fully digital, and new distribution methods began to appear. Streaming platforms emerged in Japan, offering cleaner and more stable sources. With this shift, raws no longer needed to be captured in real time. They could be extracted directly from digital streams, often at higher quality and with fewer imperfections.

This changed the balance. What had once required effort, timing, and technical knowledge became more accessible, at least for those who understood the new tools. The barrier did not disappear, but it moved.

Despite this, television recordings did not disappear. They remained relevant, and in some cases, necessary. Broadcasts were still often the first available source, appearing before official streams were accessible. Some content was only available through television, or restricted by region when distributed digitally. In these situations, the older method persisted.

These recordings, often referred to as TV rips, carried visible traces of their origin. Channel logos, slight color variations, compression artifacts, and other imperfections were part of the image. Within the community, these differences mattered. Sources began to form an informal hierarchy. Some were considered clean, taken directly from digital streams. Others were seen as less desirable, marked by the artifacts of broadcast capture.

As official distribution improved, expectations changed. Viewers became more sensitive to quality. Details that might once have been overlooked became points of discussion. The clarity of the image, the accuracy of colors, the presence of logos, and the precision of encoding all became part of how a release was evaluated.

This led to internal debates. For some, speed remained the priority. Access as quickly as possible still held value, even if the quality was not perfect. For others, the focus shifted toward fidelity. The goal was no longer simply to obtain the content, but to preserve it as accurately as possible.

This tension reflected a broader shift. The community was no longer solving the same problem. Access, while still uneven, was no longer as limited as it once had been. Instead, the focus moved toward differences in quality, presentation, and control.

At the same time, official distribution began to change in response to the very patterns these communities had established. Streaming platforms started offering episodes within hours of their original broadcast. Subtitles were provided professionally, and releases became available across multiple regions at once.

This reduced the need for traditional fansubbing, at least in its original form. The role of translating and distributing content where none existed became less central. But the activity did not disappear. It adapted.

In many cases, the focus shifted from translation to refinement. Existing subtitles were edited, corrected, or rewritten. Typesetting was improved. Visual elements were adjusted to better match the original presentation. Different sources were combined, with one providing video and another providing subtitles, to create a version that was considered more complete or more accurate.

Encoding itself became a form of craft. Decisions about compression, resolution, and color were no longer just technical requirements, but points of distinction between groups. The goal was to balance file size with visual quality, while preserving as much of the original material as possible. Different approaches emerged, and with them, different reputations.

Some groups became known for speed. Others for precision. As before, identity was tied to output.

Another important function of these communities was preservation. Not all anime remained available through official channels. Licensing agreements changed. Platforms removed content. Some series were never distributed internationally at all. In these cases, community-maintained archives became the only place where certain works continued to exist in accessible form.

This role was rarely formalized, but it was significant. The Internet allows for distribution, but it does not guarantee permanence. Content can disappear as easily as it appears. In that gap, communities often act as informal archives, maintaining copies of material that might otherwise be lost.

The relationship between these communities and the official industry has always been complex. On one side, communities helped demonstrate demand. They contributed to the growth of international audiences and made visible an interest that had previously been difficult to measure. On the other side, they operated outside legal frameworks and disrupted traditional distribution models.

Over time, the industry adapted. Faster releases, global licensing, and streaming platforms emerged, in part, as responses to these patterns. But the two systems did not merge. They continue to exist alongside each other, sometimes overlapping, sometimes in tension.

What makes anime communities particularly important is not only what they are, but what they represent.

They show that when access is limited, people do not simply wait. They build systems. When official structures improve, those systems do not disappear. They change. And when content exists, it rarely remains confined to its original boundaries.

These patterns are not unique to anime. The details, raws, fansubs, encodes, belong to a specific domain, but the structure behind them appears again and again across the Internet.

Culture moves where it can.

And once it begins to move, it does not require permission.

As these systems mature, another shift becomes visible. The same mechanisms that allow content to spread: speed, replication, shared understanding, also begin to affect something less tangible.

Not just media, but meaning.

Images, phrases, and symbols begin to circulate in similar ways. They are repeated, altered, and reinterpreted. They accumulate context. They form patterns.

And over time, they can be shaped deliberately.

This is where culture begins to change function.

It is no longer only expression.

It becomes something that can be used.

Fansub Groups, Identity, and Behavior

As fansubbing grew, certain groups began to develop recognizable identities. Names started to mean something. To someone inside the community, seeing a specific group attached to a release was enough to form expectations before even pressing play.

Some groups were known for speed. They would release episodes as quickly as possible after broadcast, sometimes within hours, occasionally with rough translation or awkward phrasing. Others took their time, focusing on accuracy, timing, and presentation. This created a quiet but persistent divide between speed and quality, and people chose sides.

Reputation followed naturally. Viewers would wait for specific groups, compare versions, and argue over which release was "correct," sometimes with surprising intensity. A single line of dialogue could spark long discussions. Not because it mattered in a practical sense, but because it mattered to the people involved.

One of the most consistent sources of debate was how much of the original Japanese language and culture should be preserved. This is where things became unexpectedly serious.

Should characters say "thank you," or "arigatou"?
Should honorifics like *-san*, *-chan*, and *-kun* be kept, or removed?

To outsiders, this might seem like a minor detail. Within the community, it could become a full argument.

Keeping honorifics was seen by some as preserving cultural nuance. Removing them was seen by others as making the dialogue more natural. Both sides believed they were improving the experience. Neither side was entirely wrong.

At times, subtitles would include translator notes explaining jokes, cultural references, or wordplay. These could appear at the top of the screen, sometimes mid-scene, occasionally breaking immersion entirely. But for many viewers, they were part of the experience. You were not just watching the show. You were being guided through it.

There was also a shared understanding, not always followed but widely recognized, that once a series became officially licensed, fansub groups would step back. This reflected an unusual balance between unofficial distribution and respect for the original creators, even if that balance was imperfect.

Despite all of this structure, the tone was not always serious.

There was humor in the process. Typos slipped through. Timing errors created unintended jokes. Overly literal translations could sound strange or unintentionally funny. And sometimes, groups would include small stylistic touches or inside jokes that only regular viewers would notice.

What emerged from all of this was not just a system for distributing content, but a culture built around interpretation, discussion, and shared effort.

People were not just watching anime.

They were participating in how it was understood.

Beyond Watching: Cultural Gravity

Anime on the Internet did not remain something people simply watched. It became something people did.

Around it, entire layers of activity formed. People began drawing characters, first by copying, then by adapting, and eventually by creating their own. Digital art communities grew around forums, early websites, and later platforms, where styles were shared, imitated, and refined. The visual language of anime, its proportions, expressions, and color palettes, began to travel independently of the shows themselves.

At the same time, other forms of participation emerged. People wrote stories, created music videos by editing scenes together, built small websites dedicated to specific characters or series, and formed communities around very narrow interests. A single show could generate dozens of micro-communities, each focused on a different interpretation, relationship, or detail.

If something exists, there is a community for it.

And in this case, those communities did not just discuss content. They extended it.

This expansion was not limited to media. It moved into behavior, language, and identity. Japanese words began appearing in everyday conversation among fans. Conventions grew, where people gathered physically, dressed as characters, and brought what had been digital culture into real space.

From there, the boundary began to shift.

Anime was often the first point of contact, but it did not remain isolated. Interest expanded outward into broader aspects of Japanese culture. Language, food, design, music, and social norms became part of the same field of curiosity.

For many, this was the first sustained exposure to a culture that had previously felt distant or inaccessible.

Japan, in particular, has often been described as a relatively closed or internally focused society, with strong cultural continuity and distinct social structures. Historically, access to that culture from the outside was limited, filtered through formal exports or selective media. The Internet changed that dynamic.

Through anime, people encountered not only stories, but fragments of everyday life. School structures, social hierarchies, forms of politeness, seasonal traditions, and unspoken rules of interaction appeared indirectly, embedded in narrative rather than explained.

This created a kind of informal cultural transmission.

It was not always accurate. It was not always complete. But it was continuous.

Over time, this exposure had real-world consequences.

People began studying the language seriously. Some traveled. Some stayed. Some built careers, relationships, and lives connected to a culture they had first encountered through compressed video files and subtitles on a screen.

This process has often been mocked, particularly in its more visible or exaggerated forms. The image of the "super-fan" became a stereotype, sometimes deserved, sometimes not.

But beneath that surface, something more significant was happening.

A form of cultural exchange had emerged that did not rely on institutions, governments, or traditional media channels. It was driven by individuals, sustained by communities, and carried through networks that were not designed for this purpose.

Distant worlds became less distant.

Not perfectly understood, not without distortion, but closer.

And in that movement, something important becomes visible.

The Internet does not just distribute information.
It changes what people are able to reach, and what they are able to become part of.

Chapter 8 – Culture II

Gaming Culture

Video games did not begin on the Internet, but they became something fundamentally different because of it.

Before widespread connectivity, games were often isolated experiences. You played alone, or with people physically present in the same room. Even when games had depth, progression, or competition, those elements existed within a closed environment. A match ended, a save file remained on a single machine, and whatever happened inside the game stayed there.

The Internet changed that by removing the boundary between the game and everything outside of it.

At first, this shift was subtle. Early online games and networked play allowed people to compete or cooperate across distance. Instead of playing against a friend sitting next to you, you played against someone in another city, or another country. This alone was enough to change the experience. Skill was no longer defined locally. It was measured against a wider, often invisible population.

Over time, this expanded into something more persistent.

Games stopped being sessions and became environments. Instead of starting and ending, they continued. Worlds existed whether you were logged in or not. Other players moved, acted, and progressed independently of you. Logging in was no longer just starting a game. It was entering a space that already existed.

This created a different kind of relationship.

Players were not only interacting with systems. They were interacting with each other, continuously. Communication became part of the structure. Chat systems, voice communication, and later external platforms allowed coordination, conflict, and social interaction to exist alongside gameplay.

From this, communities formed.

These were not always tied to a single game. They formed around genres, playstyles, or even specific roles within games. Competitive players organized around skill and ranking. Casual groups formed around shared time and familiarity. Others focused on exploration, modification, or simply existing within the world.

This last category is where something more subtle begins to appear.

In certain games, the goal is no longer clearly defined. Survival games in particular introduced systems where the objective is not to win, but to continue. You gather resources, manage hunger, avoid danger, and make small decisions that allow you to persist a little longer.

In a game like DayZ, this can mean something very simple on the surface.

You find a knife, or anything sharp enough to act like one. You cut down a bush for sticks. You start a fire. You catch a fish. You cook it. You skin an animal and use its leather. You stay warm. You stay alive.

None of this is presented as a mission. There is no clear endpoint.

And yet people will spend hours doing exactly this.

Not because they have to, but because the environment allows it.

What makes this different is not just the system, but the presence of other people inside it. You can sit in a forest, next to a fire, with someone who is not physically near you at all. Someone in another city, or another country. You can talk, wait, move slowly, or do nothing at all.

Twelve hours can pass like this.

From the outside, it may appear uneventful. Inside the experience, it is not empty. It is shared.

This is where gaming begins to overlap with something else.

The activity is simple, but the context is not. You are not just managing a character. You are spending time with another person inside a constructed space that both of you accept as real enough to act within.

This is not competition. It is not progression. It is presence.

At the same time, gaming culture began to extend beyond the games themselves.

Discussion moved to forums, early websites, and later larger platforms. Strategies were analyzed, optimized, and shared. Entire systems of knowledge formed around how games worked, often going far beyond what the developers explicitly designed.

Players documented mechanics, discovered hidden behaviors, and refined techniques.

This process led to the emergence of what is often called "meta."

The meta is not the game itself. It is the collective understanding of how the game is best played at a given moment. It changes over time as players experiment, discover new strategies, or as the game is updated.

In this sense, the game is not fixed.

It is shaped continuously by the people playing it.

This dynamic created a feedback loop between players and developers. Games were updated in response to player behavior, and players adapted in response to those updates. Over time, this became an expected part of gaming rather than an exception.

Another major shift came from the ability to modify games.

Even before official tools were provided, players began altering game files, creating new maps, mechanics, and entire experiences within existing systems. These modifications were shared online, downloaded, improved, and redistributed.

Some of these modifications became more influential than the original games.

They demonstrated that players were not only consumers of games, but contributors to them. The boundary between player and creator began to blur.

In parallel, a different kind of visibility emerged.

With the rise of streaming and recorded gameplay, playing a game became something that could be watched. This introduced a new layer to gaming culture, where performance, personality, and presentation became as important as the game itself.

People began to follow players, not just games.

This created new forms of recognition and status. Skill mattered, but so did presence. Some players became known not for being the best, but for being consistent, engaging, or simply there.

Gaming, in this sense, became both activity and observation.

At the same time, the scale of participation increased dramatically.

What had once been small communities grew into large, interconnected networks. Millions of players could engage with the same systems, the same updates, and the same spaces simultaneously.

But even at that scale, the core experience remains uneven.

Not everyone is doing the same thing. Not everyone is looking for the same outcome.

Some are competing.
Some are building.
Some are watching.

Some are simply existing inside the system.

The same game can contain all of these at once.

What connects them is not the objective of the game, but the network that allows these interactions to happen at all.

Gaming culture is not defined only by what is played, but by how people choose to inhabit it.

A game can be fast, loud, and competitive.

Or it can be quiet.

A fire in the forest.
A conversation.
Time passing between two people who are not in the same place, but are still, in some sense, together.

And in that, something becomes clear.

The Internet did not just connect games.
It turned them into spaces where people can spend time.

Before Always-Online: The LAN Era

What exists now did not appear suddenly.

Before games became persistent, global, and always available, there was a period where connection still required effort.

To understand how gaming became what it is today, it is necessary to look at a form that no longer exists in the same way.

Before gaming became permanently connected, there was a transitional phase where connection still required intention.

This took the form of local area networks, commonly known as LANs.

Instead of connecting through the global Internet, players would physically bring their computers to the same location and link them together using cables, switches, and shared infrastructure. What this created was something that was both technical and social at the same time.

You were not only playing together. You were present together.

Early LAN gatherings could be small, a few friends in a room, cables running across the floor, improvised tables, shared power strips. But as interest grew, these gatherings scaled up rapidly. What began as informal meetups became organized events, with hundreds and eventually thousands of participants bringing their own machines into a single space.

This is where something like DreamHack begins to make sense.

DreamHack started in the early 1990s as a small school gathering in Sweden. Over time, it grew into one of the largest LAN events in the world, eventually recognized for both its size and its infrastructure.

Participants would arrive with entire desktop setups. Monitors, towers, keyboards, cables. They would connect into a shared network and remain there for days. Sleeping under tables, eating irregularly, staying awake far longer than intended.

From the outside, it could look chaotic.

From the inside, it was highly structured.

What made these events unique was not just the number of people, but the concentration of computing power and connectivity in a single place. Early large-scale LANs, especially DreamHack, required infrastructure comparable to a small city.

At its peak, the event consumed massive amounts of electricity, enough to rival the usage of entire towns. Power distribution had to be carefully managed to avoid overload. Rows of computers, all running simultaneously, created both heat and demand at a scale that typical venues were not designed for.

Bandwidth became just as important.

While early LANs relied primarily on internal traffic, events like DreamHack increasingly connected to the broader Internet. At times, they operated with some of the fastest temporary network connections available anywhere in the world. This allowed not only gameplay, but large-scale data transfer between participants.

And this is where another layer appeared.

LAN events were not only about playing games. They were also about sharing data.

Files moved quickly across local networks. Games, software, media. Entire collections could be transferred in minutes that would otherwise take hours or days over slower connections at home.

This did not go unnoticed.

Swedish television at the time reported on DreamHack not only as a technological phenomenon, but as something more ambiguous. It was described as a hub for "sharing, distribution, and illegal copying," reflecting a broader uncertainty about what exactly was happening inside these events.

The response from organizers was direct.

They did not deny that data was being exchanged. Instead, they clarified their role.

They provided the infrastructure.
They kept the network running.

What participants chose to do within that network was not something they actively supervised.

This distinction is important.

It reflects a recurring pattern in the development of the Internet. The separation between infrastructure and behavior. The system enables certain actions, but does not fully control them.

LAN events existed precisely at that boundary.

They were physical gatherings built around digital interaction. Spaces where hardware, people, and networks converged in a way that was both temporary and intense. For a few days, a hall would become a concentrated version of the Internet itself.

And then it would disappear again.

What remained was not just the experience of playing games together, but the realization that connection could be scaled, shared, and intensified.

LAN culture did not last in the same form.

As home connections became faster and more stable, the need to physically gather in order to connect diminished. But something from that period carried forward.

The idea that digital interaction could still be anchored in shared time, shared space, and shared presence.

Even as the cables disappeared from the floor, the structure remained.

What began in LAN halls as informal competition did not disappear. It evolved.

Over time, competitive gaming became structured, organized, and eventually professionalized. What was once a group of players competing across rows of connected computers turned into global tournaments, teams, leagues, and audiences.

Esports is now recognized in many contexts as a form of sport. Not because of physical movement in the traditional sense, but because of the same underlying elements. Skill, training, reaction time, strategy, and competition under pressure.

The scale has changed dramatically.

Modern esports tournaments fill arenas, attract millions of online viewers, and operate with prize pools that can reach tens of millions of dollars. Professional players sign contracts, earn salaries, secure sponsorships, and in some cases build careers that extend beyond the games themselves.

What once required carrying a computer into a crowded hall is now broadcast globally in real time.

Chapter 9 – Culture III

If something exists, there is a community for it.

This is not a feature of the Internet. It is one of its defining properties.

As access expanded and more people came online, the network did not become a single shared space. It became a vast collection of smaller environments, each shaped by the people inside them. These environments could be large or small, visible or hidden, structured or chaotic. What connected them was not scale, but focus. People gathered around specific interests, identities, and ways of interacting, and over time those gatherings developed their own norms, language, and culture.

Early on, many of these spaces took the form of forums. Unlike modern platforms, forums were often independent, each with its own software, design, and community. To participate, you had to find them. There was no central system directing you there. You might arrive through a link, a recommendation, or by searching for something specific. Once inside, the experience was consistent in a way that feels unfamiliar today. Conversations were organized into threads. Users had persistent identities. Posts were not fleeting. They remained, accumulated, and could be revisited years later.

Because of this structure, identity formed differently. A username was not just a temporary label. It became associated with a history of contributions, opinions, and interactions. Over time, reputations formed. Some users became trusted sources of information. Others became known for specific behaviors or perspectives. The community itself enforced norms, sometimes explicitly through moderation, but often implicitly through shared expectations.

These forums could be broad or extremely specific. Some were dedicated to general topics such as technology or gaming. Others were focused on very narrow interests. There were communities built around particular software, obscure hobbies, or highly specialized knowledge. In many cases, these spaces were small but deeply engaged. The people participating were not just passing through. They were present, often over long periods of time.

As the Internet moved into the early 2000s, a different type of space began to emerge alongside forums. Instead of being organized purely around discussion, these platforms were built around identity and self-expression. One of the most influential was MySpace. It allowed users to create personal profiles that were not just informational, but expressive. Pages could be customized with HTML, music, colors, backgrounds, and images. For many users, especially younger ones, this was their first experience of building a public identity online.

Other platforms followed similar ideas but developed their own cultures. LiveJournal functioned as a hybrid between a blog and a social network, where users wrote long, often personal entries and formed tightly knit circles around shared interests or emotional expression. DeviantArt became a central hub for artists, where visual identity, style, and feedback loops shaped entire subcultures. Gaia Online mixed forums with avatars and virtual economies, creating a space where identity was both visual and social at the same time.

VampireFreaks was one expression of a broader pattern. It existed within a wider ecosystem of alternative social networks that catered to specific aesthetics and subcultures. Sites like Stickam focused on live video interaction before streaming became mainstream. Xanga blended blogging and social networking with a strong emphasis on personal voice. Faceparty in the UK created a youth-driven space that mixed profiles, messaging, and social discovery long before modern apps standardized the format.

These were not just websites. They were environments where people experimented with identity. Profiles were curated, exaggerated, stylized. Music taste, visual presentation, and language all became signals. For many users, especially teenagers, these platforms were formative. They were places where identity was not only expressed, but constructed.

What made these spaces distinct was that they were not yet optimized. They were messy, customizable, sometimes broken. But within that, they allowed a level of control that later platforms would reduce. A MySpace page could look completely different from another. A LiveJournal could feel like a private diary or a public performance. There was no single standard for how to exist online.

At the same time, smaller and more unusual communities continued to develop. There were penpal networks where people exchanged long messages, sometimes transitioning into handwritten letters sent across countries. There were niche forums dedicated to extremely specific topics, from obscure music genres to highly technical interests. There were communities built entirely around shared moods, aesthetics, or ideas that would not easily fit into broader platforms.

These environments required effort. You had to find them, understand them, and adapt to them. In return, they offered something different from large platforms. They offered belonging at a smaller scale.

Over time, a different model began to emerge. Instead of many independent spaces, platforms appeared that aggregated large numbers of communities into a single system. One of the most influential examples of this is Reddit. Rather than requiring users to seek out separate forums, Reddit organized communities into subgroups within a unified interface. Each subreddit functioned as its own environment, with its own rules and culture, but they were all accessible from the same place.

This changed how people moved through the Internet. Instead of belonging to one or a few spaces, users could move between many. A person might participate in dozens of communities, each with different norms and expectations. Identity became more fragmented. The same user could appear differently in different contexts, adapting to each environment rather than building a single, continuous presence.

At the same time, the scale of interaction increased. Large communities could contain millions of users. Content moved quickly. Visibility was often determined by systems of voting or algorithmic sorting rather than by long-term participation. This created a different kind of experience. It was broader, faster, and more dynamic, but often less stable.

Alongside these text-based systems, voice communication became an important part of online interaction. Platforms like TeamSpeak allowed users to connect in real time through voice channels. These spaces were often smaller and more personal. Instead of reading messages from strangers, users spoke directly to each other. Groups formed around shared activities, particularly in gaming, where coordination and communication were essential.

In these environments, presence mattered in a different way. You were not just a username attached to a post. You were a voice. People recognized each other not only by name, but by sound, tone, and behavior in real time. This created a sense of familiarity that text alone did not provide.

TeamSpeak and similar systems were not designed for mass visibility. They were designed for groups. Access was often restricted. You needed to know where to connect and who to connect with. This reinforced the idea of the Internet as a collection of separate spaces rather than a single unified environment.

In more recent years, these different models have begun to merge. Discord represents a convergence of many earlier forms. It combines elements of forums, chat systems, and voice communication into a single platform. Servers function as communities, channels organize discussion, and voice chat allows real-time interaction. Unlike earlier systems, everything exists within one interface, accessible with minimal effort.

This has made communities easier to create and join. It has also changed how they function. Persistence is built into the system. Conversations continue over time. Files, messages, and interactions accumulate in one place. At the same time, the barrier to entry is low, and movement between communities is fluid.

However, this shift has also introduced new questions. As platforms become more centralized, control becomes more visible. Decisions about moderation, access, and identity are no longer made only within individual communities, but also by the platform itself. In recent years, this has led to debates about privacy and verification. Discussions around identity verification on platforms like Discord have raised concerns about anonymity, surveillance, and the future of online interaction.

These concerns have had unexpected effects. Older systems such as TeamSpeak have seen renewed interest, particularly among users who value privacy or prefer environments with less centralized control. However, these systems were not designed for the scale of modern usage, and in some cases they have struggled to accommodate sudden increases in demand. This creates a contrast between older, more fragmented systems and newer, more integrated ones.

Across all of these environments, a consistent pattern emerges. The Internet does not present a single culture. It contains many, often existing side by side without direct interaction. A person can spend years within one set of communities and have little awareness of others that exist on the same network.

What began as a system for connecting computers has become a system for organizing people. Not into one unified space, but into many overlapping ones.

The Internet did not bring everyone together. It sorted them.

Filter Bubbles And The Traps of Modern Internet

"The Internet did not bring everyone together. It sorted them."

And once people were sorted, something else began to happen.

They stopped seeing each other.

This is where the concept of the filter bubble emerges. A filter bubble is not simply a preference or a habit. It is a structural condition created by algorithmic systems that decide what you see and what you do not. These systems use data such as your clicks, watch time, location, interactions, and even pauses to construct a model of who you are. Based on that model, they select content that you are more likely to engage with.

At first glance, this appears efficient. The system shows you what you want. But over time, this process becomes recursive.

You see something. You react to it. The system learns from that reaction and shows you more of the same. As this loop continues, the range of content narrows. Not because alternatives no longer exist, but because they are no longer shown to you.

This is not an accident. It is a design outcome.

Modern platforms are built around engagement. The more time you spend, the more valuable you are to the system. Content that aligns with your existing beliefs, preferences, and emotional responses is more likely to keep you engaged. As a result, recommendation systems tend to reinforce rather than challenge.

Over time, this creates a form of intellectual isolation. Users are increasingly exposed to information that confirms what they already think, while encountering less that contradicts it.

Closely related to this is the idea of the echo chamber. While a filter bubble is primarily driven by algorithms, an echo chamber is social. It forms when people interact mostly with others who share similar views. Within these spaces, ideas are repeated, reinforced, and amplified, often without meaningful opposition.

In practice, the two are intertwined.

Algorithms guide you toward certain content and communities. Those communities then reinforce the same perspectives. The result is a feedback loop between machine and human behavior.

Research over the past decade has shown that this interaction is complex, but consistent patterns emerge. Algorithmic personalization reduces exposure to diverse viewpoints, while social clustering increases reinforcement of shared beliefs.

One of the most studied consequences of this is polarization.

When individuals are repeatedly exposed to one-sided information, their views tend to become more extreme over time. This does not necessarily happen immediately, and not for everyone, but the effect becomes visible at scale. Recommendation systems biased toward user preferences can increase ideological polarization, particularly among those who are not strongly committed to a position beforehand.

At the same time, the structure of these systems affects how information spreads.

Content that is emotional, provocative, or controversial tends to perform better. It generates more interaction, which signals the algorithm to promote it further. This creates an environment where misinformation can spread rapidly, especially when it aligns with existing beliefs.

Within a filter bubble, false information is less likely to be challenged, not because it is convincing in an objective sense, but because the surrounding environment does not provide effective contradiction.

This has implications beyond individual understanding.

At a societal level, the fragmentation of information environments means that different groups can operate with entirely different versions of reality. Shared reference points become weaker. Public discourse becomes more difficult. Research increasingly describes this as a shift from a shared public sphere to multiple parallel ones.

However, the picture is not entirely uniform.

Some studies suggest that filter bubbles are not absolute. People are still exposed to differing viewpoints, and cross-group interaction does occur. In some cases, the Internet may even increase access to diverse information compared to traditional media.

But this exposure is often uneven and shaped by context. When opposing views do appear, they are more likely to be encountered in hostile or confrontational settings rather than constructive dialogue.

This creates another layer of distortion.

It is not only that people see less of the other side. It is that when they do, they often see it at its most extreme or least representative.

By 2026, these dynamics are no longer limited to text-based platforms. Short-form video, algorithmically curated feeds, and AI-driven recommendation systems have intensified the effect. The feedback loop has become faster, more precise, and more personalized.

The system does not just learn what you like.

It learns what keeps you.

And in doing so, it shapes not only what you see, but how you understand the world.

The Internet did not become a single global conversation.

It became many conversations happening at once, each increasingly isolated from the others, by filters.

The Echo Chambers

Once a person is consistently exposed to a narrow range of perspectives, something deeper than opinion begins to shift. It is not only what they think that changes, but how they interpret everything around them.

Echo chambers do not just reinforce beliefs. They reshape perception.

When information flows through a limited channel, the brain begins to treat that channel as representative of reality itself. Repetition plays a central role in this process. Ideas that appear frequently begin to feel more credible, not because they are verified, but because they are familiar. Over time, familiarity becomes a substitute for truth. What is repeated is trusted. What is absent is dismissed or not even considered.

This has measurable psychological effects. One of the most significant is confirmation bias, the tendency to seek out and favor information that aligns with existing beliefs. Inside an echo chamber, this bias is not only present but constantly reinforced. Each interaction, each piece of content, each agreement from others strengthens the sense that one's perspective is not just valid, but obvious.

Doubt becomes less common. Certainty becomes the default.

As certainty increases, tolerance for opposing views often decreases. Ideas that exist outside the shared framework of the group are not simply seen as different. They are more likely to be perceived as wrong, misguided, or even threatening. This shift is subtle at first, but it can become more pronounced over time, especially in environments where disagreement is discouraged or punished socially.

Another effect is emotional amplification.

Echo chambers tend to favor content that evokes strong reactions. Anger, fear, outrage, and moral judgment are more engaging than neutral information. As a result, these emotions are not only more visible, they become more common. When individuals are repeatedly exposed to emotionally charged content, their baseline emotional state can shift. What once felt extreme begins to feel normal.

This has consequences for how people interpret events outside the digital space.

If someone is regularly exposed to narratives that emphasize conflict, threat, or injustice, they may begin to perceive the physical world through the same lens. Situations are interpreted more quickly as hostile. Ambiguity is resolved in negative ways. Neutral interactions can be read as intentional or adversarial.

Over time, this can lead to a form of cognitive narrowing.

Complex issues are reduced to simplified frameworks. Nuance becomes harder to process. The world is divided into clear categories such as right and wrong, us and them, truth and deception. This simplification makes information easier to process, but it also makes it easier to misinterpret.

Social identity also becomes more tightly linked to belief.

Within an echo chamber, agreement is not only intellectual. It is social. Shared views signal belonging. Disagreement can signal separation. As a result, beliefs become tied to identity. Changing one's mind is no longer just a matter of updating information. It can feel like a loss of community or status.

This makes beliefs more resistant to change, even when confronted with new evidence.

The effects do not remain contained within the digital environment.

They extend outward into behavior, relationships, and social interaction. People carry these reinforced perceptions into conversations with family, colleagues, and strangers. Misunderstandings become more common. Discussions become more polarized. The gap between different perspectives becomes harder to bridge, not only because of disagreement, but because of fundamentally different interpretations of reality.

In some cases, this can lead to withdrawal.

If the external world does not reflect the expectations formed within the echo chamber, it may feel alien or untrustworthy. Individuals may reduce interaction with people who do not share their views, further reinforcing isolation. The digital environment becomes more comfortable than the physical one.

In other cases, the effect moves in the opposite direction.

Beliefs formed and reinforced online can motivate real-world action. This can take many forms, from changes in voting behavior and civic participation to involvement in protests, movements, or more extreme activities. The transition from online reinforcement to offline behavior is not automatic, but it becomes more likely when beliefs are both strongly held and emotionally charged.

One of the most significant long-term effects is the erosion of shared understanding.

For societies to function, there must be at least some common ground in how reality is perceived. When large groups of people operate within separate echo chambers, that common ground becomes weaker. Not because people are unwilling to communicate, but because they are starting from different premises, informed by different streams of information.

The result is not just disagreement, but fragmentation.

Different groups are not only reaching different conclusions. They are asking different questions, using different sources, and interpreting events through different frameworks. This makes consensus more difficult and increases the likelihood of conflict, both online and offline.

Echo chambers do not create these tendencies from nothing.

They amplify existing cognitive patterns and social dynamics. But by structuring how information is encountered and reinforced, they can accelerate and intensify them to a degree that becomes visible at a societal level.

What begins as a personalized stream of content can, over time, shape how individuals think, feel, and act in the world beyond the screen.

And once those patterns are established, they are not easily undone.

The Dangers of Echo Chambers

When these patterns move from internal perception to external action, the effects become visible in ways that are difficult to ignore. Echo chambers do not always lead to extreme outcomes, but when they do, the progression often follows a recognizable path. Repetition creates belief, belief creates certainty, and certainty lowers resistance to action.

Political polarization provides another example, without expanding on that topic.

A different but related pattern can be seen in cases of targeted harassment. Online communities can focus attention on specific individuals, often based on incomplete or misleading information. Once a person becomes the subject of collective attention, narratives about them can spread rapidly within the group. Because these narratives are rarely challenged within the echo chamber, they become more extreme over time. This has led to situations where individuals receive large volumes of threats, harassment, or "doxxing" attempts. In some cases, people have had to leave their homes, change jobs, or withdraw from public life entirely due to sustained online campaigns that originated in tightly clustered communities.

Financial behavior has also been influenced in similar ways. The rise of highly coordinated retail investing communities has shown how shared narratives can drive collective action in markets. While not inherently negative, there have been instances where individuals, influenced by strongly reinforced group sentiment, made high-risk financial decisions without fully understanding the consequences. In echo chamber environments, dissenting voices or warnings are often minimized, creating a perception that the group's strategy is more certain than it actually is. This has led to situations where individuals experienced significant financial loss after acting on widely shared but insufficiently examined advice.

In more extreme cases, echo chambers have been linked to radicalization. Individuals who spend extended time in highly homogeneous environments can gradually adopt more extreme positions, especially when those positions are normalized within the group. This process is often incremental. Each step feels like a small shift, but over time the cumulative effect can be substantial. There have been documented cases where individuals moved from general dissatisfaction or curiosity into more rigid and exclusionary belief systems, influenced largely by the content and interactions within specific online communities. In some instances, this has resulted in real-world violence, where actions were motivated or justified by beliefs reinforced online.

Even outside of these more visible events, the everyday effects are significant. Relationships between friends, families, and colleagues can become strained when individuals operate from different information environments. Conversations that once would have been manageable disagreements can become more difficult when each person feels that their understanding is not only correct, but supported by what they perceive as overwhelming evidence. This can lead to breakdowns in communication, reduced trust, and, in some cases, complete disengagement from those who hold different views.

What connects these examples is not a single platform or ideology, but a structure. When information is filtered, reinforced, and emotionally amplified within a closed or semi-closed environment, it can alter how individuals interpret reality. Once that interpretation becomes stable and shared within a group, it can guide decisions and actions outside the digital space.

The outcomes are not always immediate, and they are not always extreme. But when they accumulate, they shape behavior at both individual and collective levels, extending far beyond the environments where they first took form.

Chapter 10 – Memes, Meaning and Replication

Before memes became a universal language of the Internet, there were specific environments where their structure, tone, and behavior were formed.

One of the most influential of these environments was 4chan.

To understand 4chan, it is necessary to look briefly at what came before it. In the early 2000s, image boards emerged as a distinct type of online space, particularly in Japan. Platforms such as 2channel and later Futaba Channel established a format that differed from traditional forums. Instead of persistent identities and structured discussion, these boards emphasized anonymity, speed, and impermanence. Posts appeared, were responded to, and then disappeared as new content replaced them.

4chan was created in 2003 by Christopher Poole, drawing directly from these Japanese image boards. It adopted their structure almost entirely, but introduced it to an English-speaking audience at a time when most online spaces still relied on stable usernames and long-term identity.

The result was a shift in how people behaved online.

On 4chan, identity was minimal or nonexistent. Most users posted anonymously. There were no profiles to maintain, no reputations to build in the traditional sense, and little continuity between posts. Threads moved quickly and were deleted as new ones replaced them.

This created an environment where persistence was not the goal.

Ephemerality was.

Content did not need to last. It needed to spread.

Within this structure, a different kind of culture emerged. Without stable identity, expression became detached from the individual. What mattered was not who said something, but whether it resonated enough to be repeated.

This made 4chan particularly effective at producing memes.

Formats could appear, be copied, altered, and redistributed at high speed. Because there was little attachment to authorship, ideas moved freely. A single image or phrase could be picked up by dozens of users within minutes, each adding variation.

This accelerated the process of memetic evolution.

What might have taken weeks or months in other environments could happen in hours.

At the same time, the lack of identity changed the tone of interaction.

Without long-term accountability, social constraints were reduced. Humor became more extreme, more experimental, and often more transgressive. Boundaries that existed in other spaces were tested or ignored entirely.

This contributed to a style of communication that was highly influential across the Internet.

Irony became layered and unstable. Statements could be sincere, ironic, or both at the same time. Meaning was often ambiguous, requiring familiarity with the culture to interpret correctly.

This ambiguity became a defining feature of many memes that originated from or passed through 4chan.

But the same conditions that made the platform generative also made it volatile.

Anonymity allows for creativity, but it also allows for behavior that would be constrained in other environments. Without identity, there is less social cost to experimentation, but also less resistance to harmful behavior.

Content could become aggressive, offensive, or deliberately provocative.

In some cases, this was part of the culture itself. Shock, disruption, and reaction were treated as forms of participation. The goal was not always to communicate clearly, but to provoke a response.

This created a feedback loop.

Content that generated strong reactions spread more effectively. This reinforced the production of content designed to produce those reactions.

Over time, certain patterns became visible.

Ideas could be introduced, repeated, and gradually normalized within a community. Because of the speed and density of interaction, repetition occurred quickly. Exposure to the same framing, even in ironic or exaggerated forms, could accumulate.

This is where the platform intersects with something more complex.

In environments like 4chan, the distinction between humor and belief is not always stable. A concept may begin as a joke, be repeated as irony, and over time be adopted more seriously by some participants. Others may continue to treat it as humor. Both interpretations can exist simultaneously.

This creates a form of ambiguity that makes ideas difficult to evaluate from the outside.

Are they being expressed seriously, or not?

The answer is often both.

Researchers and analysts have observed that this structure can allow certain ideas to spread more easily than they would in more conventional spaces. When statements are framed as humor, they can bypass some forms of resistance. They are engaged with, repeated, and modified, even by people who do not fully endorse them.

Over time, this can shift perception.

What was once seen as extreme or outside the norm can become familiar. Familiarity reduces resistance. Repetition increases recognition. And recognition can, in some cases, lead to acceptance.

It is important to be precise here.

This does not mean that platforms like 4chan uniformly produce or promote specific beliefs.

It means that their structure allows for rapid experimentation with ideas, including those that might not spread as easily in other environments.

Some of this experimentation remains contained.

Some of it does not.

Memes created in these spaces do not stay there. They move outward, onto larger platforms, into mainstream culture, and eventually into everyday communication. As they move, they are often simplified, detached from their origin, and reinterpreted.

What began in a small, anonymous thread can become widely recognized across the Internet.

In earlier parts of the Internet, content from closed or semi-hidden communities, such as warez groups, would move outward through layers of distribution. What began in a controlled, often inaccessible environment would be repackaged, renamed, and eventually reach users who had no awareness of where it came from or how it was produced.

Memes follow a similar path.

They emerge in concentrated environments, are rapidly iterated, and then spread outward through repetition and reinterpretation. By the time they reach wider audiences, their origin is often invisible. People use them, repeat them, and understand them without ever encountering the space they came from.

The structure remains.

Only the content changes.

In this sense, 4chan functioned as a kind of cultural engine.

Not because it controlled what spread, but because it accelerated the process by which things could.

It demonstrated what happens when identity is minimized, constraints are reduced, and replication is prioritized.

The result was not a single culture, but a pattern: Fast iteration. Ambiguous meaning.

High emotional impact. And the ability for ideas to move from fringe spaces into broader awareness.

This pattern did not remain confined to one platform.

It became part of the Internet itself.

Before the Internet, culture moved through imitation, but it was difficult to observe. Ideas spread between people, changed slightly, and persisted or disappeared over time, but the process itself remained mostly invisible.

The concept of the meme was introduced by Richard Dawkins in 1976 as an analogy. He described memes as units of cultural transmission that replicate in a way comparable to genes. They vary, they are selected, and they persist based on their ability to survive within an environment.

At the time, this was speculative.

There was no way to track how ideas actually propagated across large populations in real time. The theory existed without a clear empirical substrate.

The Internet provided that substrate.

For the first time, it became possible to observe cultural replication directly. Not as an abstract concept, but as a measurable process. Images, phrases, and formats could be tracked as they appeared, spread, mutated, and either disappeared or stabilized.

What emerged confirmed part of the original analogy.

Memes behave like replicators.

They exhibit variation. A single format can produce thousands of versions, each slightly altered. They undergo selection. Some versions spread rapidly, while others fail immediately. And they demonstrate retention. Certain structures persist over long periods, even as their content changes.

Researchers in digital sociology and network science began to study these patterns more formally. Work by scholars such as Limor Shifman framed memes not just as isolated jokes, but as groups of related items that share content, form, and stance, and that are created with awareness of each other. This shifted the understanding of memes from single artifacts to systems of variation.

At the same time, computational studies began to map how memes spread through networks.

They found that meme propagation follows distributions similar to biological contagion. Most memes die quickly. A small number achieve significant spread. A very small number become dominant, appearing across multiple platforms and contexts.

This distribution is not accidental.

It reflects underlying constraints in human attention and cognition.

Research in cognitive psychology helps explain why certain memes survive. Ideas that are easier to process, more emotionally engaging, or more socially relevant are more likely to be remembered and shared. This aligns with what is sometimes called "cognitive fitness." A meme that fits well with existing mental structures has a higher chance of replication.

Humor plays a role, but it is not the only factor.

Surprise, recognition, and emotional intensity all increase transmissibility. A meme that produces a quick and clear reaction is more likely to be passed on. This is not because people consciously decide to spread it, but because it aligns with how attention works.

From a network perspective, structure matters as much as content.

Studies have shown that memes spread more effectively in clustered networks where individuals are connected through shared interests. Within these clusters, repetition reinforces visibility. Outside of them, the same meme may fail entirely.

This means that a meme is not universally effective.

It is context-dependent.

It exists within an environment that determines whether it will survive.

At this point, the biological analogy becomes more precise.

Genes do not exist in isolation. They interact with an environment. Memes behave similarly. Their success depends not only on their structure, but on the context in which they appear.

But there are limits to the analogy.

Unlike genes, memes do not have a fixed encoding. They are not stored in a stable format. They exist across multiple representations, images, text, video, and can change form while maintaining identity.

This introduces something closer to what researchers in semiotics describe as a sign system.

A meme is not just a unit of information.

It is a relationship between form and meaning that can be reinterpreted without being lost.

This is why a meme can be altered extensively and still be recognized.

Recognition does not depend on exact replication.

It depends on structural similarity.

This is where the "magic" begins to appear, not as something supernatural, but as something emergent.

A meme can propagate without centralized coordination. Thousands of individuals can produce variations of the same idea, each unaware of the others, yet contributing to a coherent pattern.

From the outside, this can look intentional.

From the inside, it feels spontaneous.

This phenomenon has been studied in the context of distributed cognition. The idea that cognitive processes are not confined to individuals, but can emerge across groups interacting through shared systems.

In this sense, a meme is not only something that spreads between people.

It is something that exists across them.

No single individual controls it, but collectively, it takes on structure.

Fringe interpretations of memetics push this further.

Some theorists have described memes as “self-organizing” or even “parasitic” structures. Not in a literal biological sense, but in the way they exploit cognitive and social mechanisms to ensure their own survival.

This language is controversial, but it highlights a real observation.

People do not always share memes because they intend to spread an idea.

They share them because the meme fits into existing patterns of thought, emotion, or identity.

The act of sharing is often automatic.

This creates a situation where replication does not require deliberate intention.

It requires alignment.

A meme that aligns with attention, emotion, and context will spread, regardless of whether the individuals sharing it understand its broader trajectory.

At scale, this produces effects that are difficult to predict.

Memes can cross cultural and linguistic boundaries with minimal adaptation. Visual formats, in particular, allow meaning to be transmitted without relying on shared language. A reaction image can convey tone across entirely different regions, as long as the underlying emotional structure is recognizable.

This gives memes a kind of efficiency that traditional communication lacks.

They compress meaning into forms that can be processed almost instantly.

This compression is not neutral.

It prioritizes speed over precision.

Subtlety is often reduced. Complexity is simplified. Nuance is replaced by recognition.

What remains is something that can move quickly.

And once something can move quickly, it begins to shape the environment it moves through.

Over time, repeated exposure to certain meme formats can influence how people interpret situations. Reactions become standardized. Certain emotional responses become more common. Language itself begins to shift, incorporating phrases and structures that originated as memes.

This is where memetics moves from description to consequence.

It is no longer only about how ideas spread.

It is about how repeated patterns of expression can influence perception.

Some studies have begun to explore this directly, examining how repeated exposure to specific types of content can alter attitudes, normalize certain viewpoints, or desensitize individuals to particular topics.

The results are not uniform, but the direction is consistent.

Repetition changes perception.

And memes are optimized for repetition.

They are not static messages.

They are systems designed, intentionally or not, to be repeated, modified, and reinserted into the flow of communication.

At this point, the original analogy becomes less metaphorical.

A meme is not just like a gene.

It is a unit of cultural evolution operating within a digital environment.

It mutates.

It competes.

It survives or disappears.

And it does so through people, but not always because of them.

The Internet did not invent this process.

It made it visible.

And once visible, it became impossible to ignore that culture itself behaves in ways that resemble a living system.

Not alive in a biological sense.

But active.

Responsive.

And capable of spreading through a population with a speed and scale that was previously impossible.

Memes As Systems

Once a meme is already in motion, it stops behaving like a single piece of content.

At scale, memes appear not as isolated images or phrases, but as clusters of variations built on a shared structure. A recognizable format, a sentence pattern, a visual template, or even a tone becomes the core. Around that core, countless versions emerge. Some are nearly identical. Others drift far enough to become something new while still remaining connected to the original.

This is where memes begin to resemble systems rather than artifacts.

Researchers have approached this idea from multiple directions. In media studies, scholars such as Limor Shifman describe memes as groups of digital items that share content, form, and stance, which are created with awareness of each other and evolve through imitation and transformation. The important shift here is that the meme is not the individual instance. It is the network of related instances.

From a computational perspective, similar patterns have been observed. Large-scale analysis of online content shows that memes propagate through variation, with certain formats acting as anchors. These anchors allow recognition, while variation allows continued engagement. Too much stability leads to stagnation. Too much change breaks recognition. Memes that persist tend to exist in a balance between the two.

This balance is not managed by any single individual.

Instead, it emerges from distributed participation. Each person who modifies or reposts a meme contributes to its trajectory, often without awareness of the larger pattern they are part of. The result is a form of collective construction where no single version is definitive, yet all versions influence what the meme becomes.

In this sense, memes function as a kind of distributed cognition.

They store and transmit shared understanding across large groups of people without requiring direct coordination. A format can carry tone, context, and implication that does not need to be explained. Recognition is enough. Meaning is compressed into structure.

This compression is part of what makes memes efficient.

A single image or phrase can contain layers of reference, built from previous iterations. To someone outside the system, it may appear trivial or opaque. To someone inside it, the meaning is immediate and often precise. Understanding depends less on explanation and more on exposure.

Another defining feature of meme systems is recursion.

Memes frequently reference themselves, their own formats, or the act of memeing. A format can become the subject of its own variation. A joke can become about the fact that it is a joke. This recursive quality allows memes to evolve not only outward, but inward, reflecting on their own structure.

Over time, patterns of lifecycle begin to emerge.

Some memes spread rapidly, saturate attention, and then disappear. Others persist in lower-intensity forms, resurfacing periodically with slight modifications. In some cases, older formats are revived and reinterpreted in new contexts, creating continuity across different periods of Internet culture.

These lifecycles are influenced by the environments in which memes circulate.

Algorithmic systems now play a significant role in shaping visibility. Content that generates interaction is more likely to be promoted, which affects which variations are seen and replicated. In this way, the evolution of memes is no longer shaped only by human preference, but also by the behavior of recommendation systems.

This introduces a second layer to the system.

Memes are selected not only by people, but by the structures that determine what people see.

The result is a hybrid process where cultural evolution and technical filtering interact continuously. A meme that aligns with both human engagement and algorithmic amplification can spread at a scale and speed that was not previously possible.

And yet, even within this increasingly structured environment, something remains difficult to fully account for.

Certain memes emerge, spread, and persist in ways that resist clear explanation. They are not always the most polished, the most meaningful, or the most intentionally created. They simply work.

They are repeated, recognized, and sustained.

Not because they were designed perfectly, but because they fit, in a way that is often only visible after the fact.

This is where the system becomes harder to reduce.

Even with models, data, and analysis, there remains an element that feels less like design and more like emergence. Patterns form, stabilize, and propagate through networks of people who are only partially aware of the role they are playing.

The meme is not the image.

It is the system that allows the image to become something more.

Memes and Magic

There is a point where the analysis begins to feel insufficient.

Even when memes are understood as systems, patterns, and structures shaped by participation and algorithms, something remains that does not sit comfortably within those explanations. Certain memes do not just spread. They feel like they arrive already formed, as if they were waiting to be discovered rather than created.

This perception is not evidence of anything supernatural, but it points to a real phenomenon. When thousands or millions of people participate in variation at the same time, outcomes can emerge that no individual intended. The result can feel coordinated, even when it is not.

This is where the experience of memes begins to take on an eerie quality.

A phrase appears in one place, then in another, then everywhere. A specific tone, image, or structure repeats across unrelated communities with slight variations, as if guided by an unseen logic. People who have never interacted produce similar versions of the same idea. Not identical, but close enough to feel connected.

It creates the impression of convergence.

In reality, this can be explained through shared context and constraints. People are exposed to similar source material, similar formats, similar cultural references. When they respond, they draw from the same pool. Under these conditions, similar outputs are not unlikely.

But the scale matters.

At small scale, coincidence feels ordinary. At large scale, it begins to feel intentional.

This is where language often shifts from description into metaphor. Memes are described as if they "want" to spread, as if they "find" the right format, as if they "adapt" to survive. These are not literal statements, but they persist because they capture something difficult to describe otherwise.

The system produces outcomes that resemble behavior.

This resemblance has led to more formal attempts to study memes beyond surface-level description. In academic contexts, memetics has drawn from evolutionary biology, cognitive science, and network theory to model how ideas replicate and stabilize. While early memetics was often criticized for being too abstract or speculative, more recent work has focused on measurable patterns such as diffusion speed, structural similarity, and network clustering.

At the same time, governments and institutional actors have taken a more practical interest.

Research into information spread, influence operations, and online behavior has increasingly included memes as a subject of analysis. This is not because memes are seen as trivial, but because they are efficient carriers of meaning. A meme can communicate alignment, humor, criticism, or ideology in a form that is quickly processed and easily shared.

Military and policy-oriented research, particularly in the United States and parts of Europe, has examined how memetic content can be used in information environments. Concepts such as "information warfare" and "psychological operations" have expanded to include not only traditional messaging, but also the organic-looking spread of cultural artifacts.

The challenge is that memes do not behave like controlled messages.

They can be introduced, encouraged, or amplified, but they cannot be fully directed. Once a meme enters circulation, it is subject to the same processes as any other. It can be altered, misunderstood, rejected, or repurposed. Attempts to control them often result in unintended variations that move in different directions.

This creates a paradox.

Memes are powerful enough to be studied, monitored, and, at times, deliberately engaged with by institutions. At the same time, they are unstable enough that no single actor can reliably determine their final form or trajectory.

From the outside, this instability can look like randomness.

From the inside, it can feel like inevitability.

Certain formats reappear across years. Certain structures seem to return even after disappearing. A style of humor fades, then resurfaces in a slightly altered form. It is not the same meme, but it is recognizably related, as if part of a longer cycle.

This recurrence adds to the sense that memes are not entirely bound to their moment.

They can persist in latent form, reactivated when conditions allow. A format that once worked can work again, not because it was preserved intentionally, but because it remains compatible with how people process and share information.

There is also a psychological dimension to this.

Humans are pattern-seeking. When we observe repeated structures across different contexts, we look for underlying causes. In environments as dense and fast-moving as the Internet, patterns appear constantly. Some are meaningful. Others are coincidental. Distinguishing between the two is not always straightforward.

Memes exist at the intersection of these tendencies.

They are shaped by human cognition, amplified by networks, and filtered by systems that prioritize engagement. When all of these forces align, the result can feel disproportionate to any single cause.

A simple image becomes widely recognized. A phrase becomes embedded in everyday language. A format becomes a shared reference point across communities that have no direct connection to each other.

Chapter 11 – (The battle for) Control

Was control ever absent to begin with on the internet?

It is easy to imagine, especially in its earlier form, as something open, neutral, and uncontrolled. A space where people could speak freely, where information moved without interference, where communication existed without direction.

But this idea does not hold for long when examined.

Every system that allows communication also creates the possibility of influence. The moment information can move between people, it can be shaped, emphasized, repeated, or suppressed. Not always deliberately, not always visibly, but inevitably.

Control does not need to begin as a plan.

It can begin as a property.

A system that distributes information will always raise the question of who decides what is seen, what is heard, and what is ignored. Even in the absence of formal authority, patterns emerge. Some voices become louder. Some ideas spread further. Some structures guide attention without appearing to do so.

In this sense, control is not something that was added later.

It is something that was always possible.

The early Internet is often remembered as a place without control. And in some ways, compared to what exists now, it was less structured, less centralized, less visible in how influence operated.

But it was not empty of it.

Moderators existed. Communities enforced norms. Access required knowledge. Visibility depended on where you were and who you knew. Even then, information did not move evenly. It followed paths shaped by people, systems, and limitations.

What has changed is not the existence of control, but its form.

It has shifted from something that was often visible and local, into something that is increasingly distributed, embedded, and difficult to isolate. It no longer always appears as a rule or a restriction.

It appears as flow.

As what reaches you.
As what repeats.

As what seems common.

And because of this, the question is no longer simply whether control exists.

But how it operates.

And whether it can still be recognized at all.

Before the Internet Control Was Centralized

Before the Internet, control over information was not hidden. It was structured, visible, and largely centralized.

Communication systems were limited in number and expensive to operate. Printing presses, radio transmitters, and television networks required infrastructure, licensing, and coordination. As a result, only a relatively small number of institutions had the ability to distribute information at scale. Newspapers were edited before publication. Broadcasts were scheduled and curated. Content passed through layers of decision-making before it reached the public.

This created a system of gatekeepers.

Editors decided what was newsworthy and how it should be presented. Broadcasters determined what would be aired and when. Governments, depending on the country and time period, could exert direct or indirect influence over what was allowed, restricted, or promoted. Even in systems that valued press freedom, access to mass communication was never evenly distributed. It was concentrated.

Control, in this environment, was not subtle.

It could be identified. It could be questioned. It could be resisted, but it was rarely invisible. If something did not appear in a newspaper, there was a place to look for the decision behind that absence. If a broadcast followed a certain narrative, it could often be traced back to a known source or institution.

At the same time, this concentration created limitations. Information moved more slowly. Perspectives were narrower. Entire topics could remain underrepresented or ignored simply because they did not pass through the available channels. The system was stable, but constrained.

This does not mean it was entirely controlled in a uniform way. Different countries operated under different conditions. Some environments allowed for competing publications and viewpoints, while others were more tightly regulated. But even in the most open systems, the structure remained similar. A limited number of voices had the ability to reach large audiences, and those voices operated within identifiable frameworks.

The public, in turn, consumed information in a more linear way. You read what was printed. You watched what was broadcast. There were fewer opportunities to respond, fewer ways to participate directly in shaping the flow of information. Communication was largely one-directional.

This created a clear distinction between those who produced information and those who received it.

Control existed within that distinction.

It was not total, and it was not always intentional in every instance, but it was built into the structure of the system itself. The ability to decide what would be seen, when it would be seen, and how it would be framed was concentrated in relatively few hands.

What the Internet would later change was not the existence of control, but the visibility of it. And, more importantly, who could participate in it.

The Early Internet And The Illusion of Freedom

When the Internet began to enter public use, it appeared to break this structure.

For the first time, the ability to publish and distribute information was no longer limited to institutions with physical infrastructure. A website could be created by an individual. A forum could be started by a small group. Communication could happen directly between people without passing through traditional gatekeepers.

This created a strong impression of openness.

Compared to previous systems, it felt uncontrolled. There were fewer barriers to entry, fewer visible layers of approval, fewer centralized points where decisions were made before information reached others. People could write, share, and respond in ways that had not been possible before.

But this did not mean control disappeared.

It changed form.

In place of centralized gatekeepers, smaller structures emerged. Forums had administrators and moderators. Communities developed rules, both explicit and implicit. Access still depended on knowledge. You needed to know where to go, how to connect, how to navigate systems that were not always intuitive.

Information did not spread evenly. It moved through networks of people who were already connected in some way, through shared interests, shared spaces, or shared technical understanding. Visibility was still shaped, but now it was shaped locally rather than globally.

Influence became more fragmented.

Instead of a few institutions shaping large audiences, many smaller groups shaped smaller ones. Each community developed its own norms, its own language, its own boundaries. What was visible in one space might be completely absent in another. The Internet did not create a single shared environment. It created many overlapping ones.

This fragmentation contributed to the feeling of freedom.

Because there was no single authority directing everything, it felt as though there was no control at all. But what existed instead was a distributed system of influence. Control was not removed, it was dispersed.

It also required effort.

To find information, you often had to look for it. To participate, you had to engage actively. There was no single feed presenting everything at once. The experience was shaped by where you chose to go and who you interacted with.

This created a different relationship between the user and the system.

You were not only receiving information. You were navigating toward it.

And because of this, control was less visible.

It existed in the structure of communities, in the flow of discussion, in the norms that developed over time. It was not imposed from a single point, but it was still present in how information moved, how it was framed, and how it was understood.

What made this period distinct was not the absence of control, but the perception of its absence.

Platforms Change Everything

The structure shifts again with the rise of large platforms.

What was once fragmented begins to consolidate. Instead of navigating between independent websites, forums, and communities, users increasingly operate within a small number of centralized systems. These platforms provide everything in one place. Communication, content, identity, distribution.

This changes how information moves.

On earlier parts of the Internet, visibility depended on where you went. Now, it depends on what is shown to you. The user no longer searches in the same way. The system presents. Content arrives through feeds, timelines, recommendations. The flow becomes continuous.

At the center of this shift is a different kind of control.

Not editorial in the traditional sense, and not entirely manual. Instead, it is algorithmic. Systems determine what appears based on patterns. Past behavior, interactions, engagement, similarity to other users. The criteria are not always visible, and they are constantly changing.

This does not feel like control in the traditional sense.

There is no single decision that can be pointed to. No editor choosing one story over another in a way that can be easily identified. Instead, there is a process. Automated, adaptive, and distributed across millions of interactions.

But the effect is similar.

Some things are seen more than others. Some ideas spread further. Some content is amplified, while other content remains largely unseen. The difference is that this selection is now embedded in the system itself.

A single piece of content can reach millions of people within hours. The boundaries between communities become less defined. Information moves faster, further, and with less friction. The distinction between producer and audience becomes less clear, as anyone can contribute, but not everything will be equally visible.

The new dynamic is that visibility becomes the central resource.

Not just the ability to publish, but the ability to be seen. And because visibility is determined by systems that optimize for engagement, the type of content that spreads begins to shift. Material that attracts attention, that provokes reaction, that encourages interaction, is more likely to be promoted.

This is not necessarily intentional in a directed sense.

It is a result of how the systems are designed.

But it changes the environment.

Control becomes less about restricting what can be said, and more about influencing what is likely to be noticed. The system does not need to remove information if it can simply make other information more prominent.

And because this process operates continuously, at scale, and without a single visible point of decision, it becomes harder to recognize.

The user experiences it as a stream. But that stream is shaped.

Not by one hand, but by a system designed to select, prioritize, and repeat.

Who Wants Control?

As the structure of the Internet changes, the question of control becomes very complex.

It is no longer concentrated in a small number of visible institutions, and it is no longer absent in the way it may have seemed in earlier stages. Instead, it becomes something that multiple actors pursue at the same time, often for different reasons, using different methods, and operating at different scales.

Governments are one of those actors.

Their interest in control is not new. States have always had reasons to shape information, whether to maintain stability, influence public opinion, or respond to external pressures. What changes with the Internet is the environment in which this takes place. Information moves faster, crosses borders more easily, and can originate from anywhere. This creates both an opportunity and a challenge. Control is harder to enforce in a traditional sense, but new tools emerge that allow influence to be applied in more subtle and distributed ways.

Corporations are another.

For them, the motivation is often tied to attention and economics. Platforms operate on engagement. The more time users spend within a system, the more valuable that system becomes. This creates an incentive to shape what is shown in ways that keep users present, interacting, and returning. The goal is not always to control what people think, but to influence what they see, what they respond to, and how long they remain within the environment.

Political groups and organized movements also operate within this space.

For them, the Internet provides a way to reach large audiences without relying on traditional channels. Messaging can be distributed directly, repeated across networks, and adapted in real time. Narratives can be reinforced, challenged, or reshaped through coordinated effort. What once required access to broadcast infrastructure can now be attempted through distributed systems of communication.

There are also less formal actors.

Communities, interest groups, and individuals who participate in shaping discourse, sometimes intentionally, sometimes simply through repeated behavior. Influence does not always require organization. Patterns can emerge from collective action, even when that action is not centrally directed.

Visibility matters. Attention can be directed. Repetition can reinforce ideas.

The Internet does not require control to be total in order to be effective. It only requires that certain patterns become more prominent than others.

And because the system allows many participants to act at once, control is no longer something held by one entity.

It becomes something contested.

Different actors, with different goals, operating within the same environment, shaping the same flows of information, often without directly interacting with each other.

The result is not a single controlled system.

It is a field of influence.

Where multiple forces attempt to guide what is seen, what is believed, and what continues to circulate.

The Industrialization of Influence

At a certain point, influence stops being incidental.

It becomes organized.

What was once the result of individuals speaking, sharing, and interacting begins to take on a different form. Structured efforts emerge, designed to participate in the flow of information, and to shape it deliberately and at scale.

This is where influence becomes industrial.

There are now entire groups, teams, and organizations whose role is to operate within the Internet in ways that resemble ordinary users, while working toward specific outcomes. These can take many forms. Coordinated posting. Repeated messaging. Content designed to appear organic, but produced with intent.

The scale of this activity is massive.

Across different countries and contexts, there are documented cases of organizations employing large numbers of people to engage in online discourse. Some produce articles, videos, or commentary aligned with particular narratives. Others operate more directly within platforms, posting on forums, responding to discussions, amplifying certain viewpoints, or introducing new ones.

In some instances, this work is tied to state interests. Organizations have been identified that specialize in online influence operations, employing staff to create and distribute content across multiple platforms. The goal is not always to convince directly, but to shape the environment. To introduce doubt, reinforce certain ideas, or make particular perspectives appear more common than they are.

In other cases, the activity is commercial.

Companies hire teams to promote products, manage perception, or influence public opinion around brands. Content can be generated in large volumes, distributed through networks of accounts, and designed to blend into normal user activity. The distinction between genuine expression and strategic messaging becomes less clear.

This does not always rely on automation.

While automated systems exist, a significant portion of this activity is carried out by real people. Individuals who post, comment, and interact in ways that are difficult to distinguish from ordinary participation. The effectiveness of this approach comes from its integration into existing spaces. Forums, comment sections, social platforms, all become environments where influence can be applied without being immediately visible.

Content is produced, distributed, and reinforced as part of ongoing effort. Narratives are maintained over time. Messages are repeated across different contexts, adapting slightly to fit each environment while preserving a core structure.

And because this activity operates within the same systems as everyday communication, it does not always stand out.

It appears as part of the normal flow, comments, posts, videos etc.

Individually, these may not seem significant.

But collectively, they form patterns.

And those patterns shape perception.

Not by forcing a conclusion, but by influencing what seems familiar, what seems common, and what appears to be shared by others.

This is where control becomes difficult to locate.

Culture as a Battleground

As influence becomes organized and continuous, it does not remain confined to obvious forms such as news, statements, or direct argument.

It merges into culture.

This shift is subtle, but significant. Culture is where ideas are carried without needing to present themselves as ideas. It exists in humor, in language, in references, in the way people speak and respond without necessarily analyzing why.

Memes, phrases, and formats become part of this.

They are repeated, shared, slightly altered, and reintroduced across different spaces. At first, they may appear trivial. A joke, an image, a line of text. But repetition gives them weight. Familiarity makes them easier to accept, easier to reuse, easier to pass along.

This is where influence changes form.

Instead of presenting a position directly, it can be embedded within something that appears neutral or entertaining. A message does not need to be argued if it can be absorbed indirectly. It can move through humor, through irony, through shared language that does not feel like instruction.

Because of this, culture becomes a space where influence is both effective and difficult to isolate.

There is no clear boundary between what is intentional and what is organic. A phrase can begin in one context and spread into another. A format can be adopted, reshaped, and reused by people who are not aware of its origin. Meaning can shift as it moves, but certain underlying patterns remain.

This makes culture a useful medium.

It does not require attention in the same way direct information does. It does not ask to be evaluated. It is encountered, repeated, and internalized over time. The more it appears, the more it feels familiar. The more familiar it feels, the less it is questioned.

At scale, this creates an environment where ideas can circulate without needing to be presented as arguments.

They become part of how people communicate.

And because culture is participatory, this process is not limited to those who initiate it. Once a pattern enters circulation, it can be carried forward by anyone. Repeated without intent, adapted without awareness, reinforced through use.

This is what makes it difficult to distinguish where influence begins and where it simply continues.

Culture provides a highway that is persistent, adaptable, and often invisible to those within it.

The User as Both Target and Participant

Within this system, the role of the individual becomes less clear.

It is easy to think of influence as something that moves in one direction. From those who shape information to those who receive it. But the structure of the Internet does not support a purely one-way model.

The same systems that expose people to information also allow them to redistribute it.

A user reads, watches, or encounters something, and then reacts. A comment is written. A post is shared. A phrase is repeated. In doing so, the user becomes part of the process that determines what continues to circulate.

This creates a dual position.

The individual is both influenced and influencing.

Not necessarily in a deliberate sense, but through participation. Every interaction contributes to the visibility of something. Every repetition extends its reach. The system does not distinguish between intentional amplification and casual engagement. It registers activity, and that activity becomes part of what shapes the flow.

Because of this, influence does not need to be fully directed from above.

It can propagate through ordinary behavior.

A message does not need to be believed to be spread. It only needs to be interacted with. Agreement, disagreement, humor, criticism, all of these can contribute to visibility. The distinction between support and opposition becomes less important than the fact that attention has been given.

This creates a situation where participation itself becomes a mechanism.

The more something is engaged with, the more it appears. The more it appears, the more likely it is to be engaged with again. Over time, this produces patterns that can feel organic, even when they are influenced by underlying structures or initial direction.

For the individual, this can be difficult to recognize.

There is no clear moment where one transitions from observer to participant. The shift happens through action, often small and unremarkable. A response, a share, a repetition. Each one seems isolated, but collectively they contribute to something larger.

This is what makes the system self-reinforcing.

Influence does not rely solely on those who initiate it. It relies on those who carry it forward, whether intentionally or not.

And because everyone has the ability to participate, everyone becomes part of the environment that shapes what is seen, what is repeated, and what remains in circulation.

This creates something that begins to resemble a shared system of awareness.

Not consciousness in any literal or biological sense, but a continuous, interconnected field of interaction. Millions of individuals, observing, reacting, repeating, and modifying information in real time. Each action is small on its own, but collectively they form patterns that move across the network.

The Internet, in this sense, begins to function less like a collection of separate users and more like a system where responses accumulate.

What appears, what spreads, what persists, is shaped by this accumulation.

Because everything is connected through shared platforms and overlapping spaces, signals do not remain isolated. A post in one place can influence discussion in another. A phrase can move across communities. A pattern can emerge without a central point of origin.

This gives rise to an effect that feels larger than any individual contribution.

Something closer to a collective process.

Not unified or consistent, but interconnected.

And this process does not remain contained within the network.

What circulates online begins to affect what happens outside of it. Language changes. Perceptions shift. Decisions are influenced. Actions are taken. The boundary between digital interaction and physical reality becomes less distinct, not because the two are the same, but because they continuously inform each other.

In this way, the Internet does not simply reflect the world.

It participates in shaping it.

Through accumulation, through repetition, and through the constant interaction of individuals who are both observing and contributing at the same time.

Algorithmic Control and Filter Loops

Within this interconnected system, another layer operates continuously in the background.

Selection.

Not everything that exists within the network is shown. Not everything that is shown is seen equally. Between what is created and what reaches the individual, there is a process that determines visibility.

This process is largely algorithmic.

Systems analyze behavior, interactions, timing, and patterns, then decide what to present. The goal is not framed as control, but as relevance. Content is selected based on what is most likely to be engaged with, what is most likely to hold attention. Commercialism and capitalism is of course a strong driving force behind this result too, money needs to be made and somebody is going to have to pay for hardware and server costs.

But over time, this creates a feedback loop.

What a person sees influences how they respond. That response is measured, and similar content is shown again. Gradually, the range of visible information narrows, not because other content disappears, but because it is no longer prioritized.

The system adapts.

And in doing so, it begins to shape the environment each user experiences.

Two individuals can exist within the same platform and encounter entirely different versions of it. Different topics, different tones, different perspectives. Each one feels complete from the inside, but partial when viewed from the outside.

This is where control becomes difficult to recognize.

There is no instruction being given. No direct message telling someone what to think. Instead, there is a continuous adjustment of what is visible, what is repeated, and what is absent. Of course if you would have the power to adjust what is seen, you could put the odds in your favor.

Over time, repetition creates familiarity.

Familiarity creates acceptance.

And acceptance influences interpretation.

The system does not need to convince. It only needs to present certain patterns more often than others.

Because within the flow of information, what appears frequently begins to feel normal. And what feels normal is less likely to be questioned.

This is how influence can operate without direct direction.

Not by limiting what exists, but by shaping what is encountered.

And because this process is continuous, adaptive, and largely invisible, it becomes part of the environment itself, not something separate from the Internet, but something that is currently being built into how it functions for many users.

Can the Internet Really Be Controlled

There is no single system, no single authority, no central point that governs everything at once. The Internet is too large, too distributed, too varied in its structure for total control to exist in a traditional sense. Information can move across borders, across platforms, across systems that do not fully align with each other.

But this does not mean it is uncontrolled because control exists in fragments.

Platforms control what is visible within their systems. Governments regulate access, enforce laws, and in some cases restrict or shape information flows within their borders. Organizations and groups influence discourse within the spaces they occupy. Individuals contribute to patterns through their own behavior.

Each of these operates within its own scope.

None of them are absolute.

This creates a situation where control is not centralized, but layered.

Different actors influence different parts of the system. Their effects overlap, sometimes reinforcing each other, sometimes conflicting. A piece of information may be amplified in one space and suppressed in another. A narrative may dominate one platform and remain largely invisible on another.

From the perspective of the user, this can appear inconsistent.

What is visible depends on where you are, what systems you are within, and how those systems are configured. There is no single version of the Internet that everyone experiences in the same way.

This makes the idea of total control difficult to apply.

No single actor can fully determine what exists across the entire network. But many actors can shape what is experienced within specific parts of it.

Control, in this sense, becomes partial.

And continuous.

It is not something that is achieved once and maintained permanently. It requires ongoing effort, adaptation, and response to changes in the system. As platforms evolve, as users change behavior, as new technologies emerge, the methods of influence shift as well.

What exists is not a stable state of control.

But a dynamic process.

An environment where different forces attempt to guide, shape, and influence what is seen, without ever fully determining it.

And because of this, the question is not only whether the Internet can be controlled.

But how much control is enough to matter.

If control is partial and constantly shifting, the question of who wins does not have a clear answer. There is no final state where one actor takes control of the Internet and keeps it. The system changes too quickly, and too many forces act within it at the same time. Instead of a winner, there is accumulation. Some actors gain influence for a period, then lose it. Platforms rise and fall. Narratives spread, fade, and are replaced. What matters is not permanent control, but temporary visibility, the ability to shape what is seen in a given moment. Even then, influence does not disappear when it weakens. It leaves traces in language, in culture, in memory, and can return in new forms. The result is not a single outcome, but a layered one, where many forces shape the environment at once without fully controlling it. For the individual, there is no single source behind everything, only overlapping influences, some visible, others built into the system itself. The Internet is not something that can be won. It is something that is continuously shaped.

Chapter 12 – The Dead Internet Theory

The modern Internet is no longer shaped only by people.

It is shaped by systems, automation, and scale. Millions of interactions occur every second, but not all of them originate from human intent. Automated accounts generate clicks, views, and engagement. Content is produced, repeated, and amplified in ways that are difficult to trace back to a single source. These systems are used commercially to drive visibility, influence purchasing decisions, and increase engagement. They are also used politically, to promote narratives, reinforce positions, and in some cases contribute to tension between groups.

Within this environment, a question begins to emerge.

How much of what is online is actually human.

This is where the idea known as the Dead Internet Theory appears.

The Dead Internet Theory is not a proven claim, but a speculative interpretation of observable trends. It suggests that a significant portion of online activity is no longer driven by real individuals, but by automated systems generating and interacting with content at scale. According to this view, much of the Internet has become a space where artificial activity dominates, while human presence is less visible than it appears.

The theory did not originate in formal research. It emerged from online discussions, particularly in forums, where users began to notice patterns that felt inconsistent with organic behavior. Repeated phrasing, identical responses across different accounts, unusual engagement patterns, and content that seemed designed more for algorithms than for people.

Automated systems, often referred to as bots, are widely used across the Internet. They can perform actions such as posting content, liking posts, following accounts, and generating traffic. In commercial contexts, bots are used to inflate engagement metrics, promote products, or manipulate visibility. In political contexts, coordinated networks of accounts have been used to amplify specific messages or create the appearance of consensus.

In addition to bots, there are large-scale content generation systems.

Search engine optimization has led to the production of vast amounts of low-quality or repetitive content designed primarily to rank in search results rather than to provide meaningful information. More recently, advances in artificial intelligence have made it possible to generate text, images, and video at scale, further increasing the volume of non-human content.

This creates an environment where distinguishing between human and automated activity becomes more difficult.

The Dead Internet Theory began to circulate more clearly in the early 2020s, although the observations behind it are older. It did not emerge from a single source, but from scattered discussions across forums, imageboards, and niche communities where users began comparing experiences. The common thread was not a single claim, but a shared unease. Something about the Internet felt different, but difficult to define precisely.

People pointed to subtle changes first. Search results becoming increasingly repetitive, with multiple pages saying the same thing in slightly different ways. Comment sections that appeared active but lacked variation in tone or perspective. Social media feeds that felt dense with content, yet strangely uniform in structure and language. The sense was not that activity had decreased, but that it had become less distinct.

From there, more specific patterns were discussed. Accounts that posted at regular intervals without interruption, across time zones, with no visible signs of fatigue. Conversations where responses appeared quickly but did not fully engage with what was said. Threads that gained traction rapidly, then stabilized into predictable repetition rather than evolving discussion. None of these observations were individually conclusive, but together they formed a pattern that users began to notice more consistently.

Another point of focus was the shift in content itself. Large volumes of material appeared to be produced not to communicate, but to occupy space. Articles structured around keywords rather than ideas. Videos following identical formats regardless of topic. Posts designed to trigger engagement without adding new information. The Internet began to feel less like a place of exchange and more like a system maintaining its own activity.

Another point of focus was the shift in content itself. Large volumes of material appeared to be produced not to communicate, but to occupy space. Articles structured around keywords rather than ideas. Videos following identical formats regardless of topic. Posts designed to trigger engagement without adding new information. The Internet began to feel less like a place of exchange and more like a system maintaining its own activity.

In response to this, some users have begun experimenting with ways to access an earlier version of the web's informational landscape. One commonly shared method involves using date-restricted search queries, such as adding terms like "before:2020" in Google Search, to filter results to content published prior to the widespread rise of large-scale AI-generated material and aggressive search optimization. While not a perfect solution, this approach is often described as a way to approximate an older snapshot of search results, where content may feel less uniform and less systemically amplified.

As these observations accumulated, the interpretation followed. The theory proposed that the visible layer of the Internet had become increasingly synthetic, not entirely devoid of human presence, but supplemented to such an extent that the overall environment no longer reflected purely human interaction.

As these observations accumulated, the interpretation followed. The theory proposed that the visible layer of the Internet had become increasingly synthetic, not entirely devoid of human presence, but supplemented to such an extent that the overall environment no longer reflected purely human interaction. The idea was not necessarily that people had disappeared, but that their signal had become diluted within a growing volume of generated and automated content.

What gave the theory persistence was not evidence of total replacement, but consistency of experience. Different users, in different spaces, reported similar impressions without coordination. A sense of artificial density. Of interaction that continued, but did not always feel grounded in individual presence. The Internet appeared full, but not always alive in the way it once had been.

There are measurable elements behind these perceptions. The growth of automated accounts, the expansion of content generation systems, the optimization of platforms for engagement rather than originality. These factors contribute to an environment where repetition, amplification, and volume become more prominent than distinct expression.

But the theory itself extends beyond measurement.

It attempts to describe a qualitative shift.

Not whether the Internet is literally dead, but whether the nature of interaction has changed to the point where it no longer feels entirely human. Whether the patterns that emerge are driven more by systems than by individuals. Whether activity can continue indefinitely, even as the sense of presence becomes less certain.

This is why the theory remains difficult to resolve.

It is not a claim that can be easily proven or disproven in absolute terms.

It is a description of a feeling, supported by observations, shaped by interpretation, and reinforced by the experience of those who encounter the same patterns across different parts of the network.

The Silent Internet

Even without assuming that most of the Internet is artificial, something has undeniably changed in how it feels to be online. One of the simplest explanations is also one of the least discussed. Most people do not actively participate. They read, watch, scroll, and leave without interacting. For every visible comment or post, there are many more silent observers. This creates an imbalance where activity appears high, but direct human expression can be relatively thin. The space looks full, but much of that presence is passive.

At the same time, the structure of the Internet has shifted away from many small, distinct communities into a smaller number of large platforms. Earlier spaces often had strong identities, slower conversations, and recognizable participants. Now, interaction is spread across systems where content moves quickly and identity is less stable. This reduces variation. Different places begin to feel similar. The edges between communities soften, and with that, some of the distinctiveness disappears. The Internet becomes broader, but flatter.

Another noticeable change is how difficult it has become to trace the origin of content. The same ideas, phrases, and formats appear in multiple places at once, often detached from any clear source. Something appears, spreads, is reshaped, and reappears again without a visible starting point. This gives the impression that content exists independently of the people who created it. Not because creators are absent, but because the connection between creation and distribution has weakened.

Time behaves differently as well. Trends rise and disappear quickly. Conversations rarely build over long periods. Instead of developing, they reset. The same topics return in cycles, often with similar language, similar arguments, and similar outcomes. This creates a sense of repetition, not always exact, but close enough to feel familiar. The Internet feels active, but not always progressive.

There is also a reversal in how content appears. It no longer always begins with a person wanting to express something. In many cases, content exists first, and people react to it. Systems produce, suggest, and circulate material continuously, and human interaction follows. This shifts the role of the individual from creator to responder more often than before.

Underlying all of this is a strong economic incentive. Visibility, engagement, and attention have measurable value. This encourages the production of content at scale, the repetition of successful formats, and the optimization of material for reach rather than originality. The result is an environment where what spreads is not always what is most meaningful, but what performs best within the system.

For the individual, this creates a subtle psychological effect. It becomes harder to tell what is genuine. Not in a dramatic sense, but in small moments. A comment that feels slightly off. A conversation that does not fully connect. A sense that interaction is happening, but not always between clearly identifiable people. This does not mean that others are not present. It means that presence is less certain.

This uncertainty contributes to a feeling that is difficult to describe directly. The Internet still functions. It is still active, still populated, still constantly moving. But something about the texture of interaction has shifted. It can feel less grounded, less distinct, more repetitive, more automated, even when real people are involved.

In that sense, the Dead Internet Theory does not need to be entirely true to resonate.

It only needs to describe something that people recognize.

Not an absence of activity, but a change in its nature. Not a disappearance of people, but a dilution of their presence within a system that now produces, repeats, and sustains itself at a scale that no longer depends entirely on them.

The Internet is not dead.

But it is no longer only alive in the way it once was.

Chapter 13 – Reality

Over time, the role of the Internet has shifted from something separate from reality into something that actively shapes it. It was once understood as a place you entered and left, a tool used for communication, information, or entertainment, with a clear boundary between being online and being in the physical world. That boundary has gradually weakened. What happens online now influences how people think, act, and understand the world around them, and the effects do not remain contained within the network.

For many, the Internet is no longer a destination but a constant presence. It runs alongside everyday life, filling moments, providing context, and continuously updating what is visible and relevant. This changes how reality is experienced, because much of what people know about the world does not come from direct experience, but from what they encounter through screens. News, opinions, reactions, and interpretations arrive through the same channels, often blended together, making it less obvious where one ends and another begins.

Media has always influenced perception, but the difference now lies in scale and speed. Information is constant, responsive, and personalized. Two people can live in the same place and still experience very different versions of the world based on what they are exposed to. What feels immediate and important to one person may barely exist in the awareness of another. This does not remove reality, but it fragments how it is perceived.

At the same time, experiences that occur online are not separate from reality in any meaningful sense. Conversations, relationships, conflicts, and communities that exist through digital interaction carry real emotional and social weight. The medium changes the form, but not the impact. A message can affect someone as directly as a spoken word, and interactions that happen across distance can shape behavior in physical space.

This creates a layered experience of reality. The physical world remains constant and tangible, but it is increasingly interpreted through a digital layer that is always present. Events move between these layers, recorded, shared, discussed, and then returned to the physical world through decisions and actions. What begins in one space often continues in the other, forming a continuous loop rather than separate domains.

Another change is how memory is formed and maintained. In earlier forms of experience, memory depended largely on what a person directly saw, heard, and retained over time. Now, events are recorded, stored, and replayed continuously. Moments can be revisited, reinterpreted, and reshared long after they occur. This creates a form of external memory that exists outside the individual, persistent and accessible, but also subject to framing and selection. What is remembered is no longer only what was experienced, but what is recorded and circulated.

This also affects how significance is assigned. Events that are widely shared can feel more important, while those that remain unrecorded or unseen may feel less real, regardless of their actual impact. Visibility begins to influence perceived importance. What appears repeatedly gains weight, while what does not appear can fade, even if it exists in the physical world.

At the same time, presence itself becomes observable. Activities, locations, and interactions can be documented and displayed in real time, turning parts of everyday life into something that is not only experienced but also presented. This introduces a subtle shift where moments are not only lived, but also considered in terms of how they appear to others. The experience and the representation of the experience begin to exist together.

As a result, understanding the world becomes more dependent on access and exposure. People rely on different sources, encounter different patterns of information, and form perspectives based on what reaches them. This does not eliminate truth, but it changes how consistently it is seen. The same event can be interpreted in multiple ways depending on how it is presented and where it appears.

The Internet also changes the nature of presence. A person can exist physically in one place while participating in many others at the same time. Interaction is no longer limited by location, and attention is divided across multiple contexts. This expands the range of experience but also disperses it, making reality something that is no longer confined to a single setting.

None of this makes the world less real. Instead, it expands what reality includes. Digital interaction becomes part of how people experience and respond to the world, influencing perception, behavior, and decision-making. The Internet does not replace reality, but it reshapes how it is accessed and understood.

At this point, the distinction between online and offline becomes less meaningful. What matters is how they interact, because they no longer exist independently.

At the same time, a quieter shift has begun to appear in the opposite direction. As the Internet has become more constant, more integrated, and more difficult to separate from daily life, some people have started to step back from it. Not entirely, but deliberately. There is a growing awareness of how much time, attention, and perception is shaped by continuous connection, and with that, a desire to regain some distance from it.

This takes different forms. Some reduce their use of social media or leave certain platforms entirely. Others limit when and how they connect, creating boundaries that did not previously exist. The idea of being offline, once an inconvenience, begins to feel intentional. Not a lack, but a choice.

Alongside this, there is renewed interest in physical media. Music stored on discs or files that cannot be removed or altered remotely. Films owned rather than accessed. Books that exist independently of updates, licenses, or availability. The appeal is not only nostalgia, but stability. A sense that what you have remains yours, unchanged by decisions made elsewhere.

Devices themselves reflect this shift. Simpler phones, often referred to as "dumb phones," are chosen not because they offer more, but because they offer less. Fewer distractions, fewer points of connection, fewer layers between the individual and their immediate environment. What was once considered outdated becomes, for some, a way to reduce noise.

This movement does not replace the Internet, and it does not reverse its role. But it introduces a counterbalance. A recognition that constant connection is not the only way to exist within the modern world. That it is possible to step back, even partially, and experience something closer to a slower, more direct form of reality.

In this sense, the trajectory is not one-directional. As systems become more advanced and more integrated, there is also a parallel movement toward simplicity, ownership, and control over one's own attention.

The two exist at the same time.

And the choice between them, at least for now, remains open.

Chapter 14 – Weaponization

At a certain point, communication stops being neutral, not because the systems themselves change, but because of how they are used. The Internet was built to move information quickly across distance, but that same capability allows it to be used not only for sharing and expression, but for influence with intent. This does not rely on physical presence or traditional forms of conflict. Instead, it operates through perception, shaping how people understand events, how they interpret information, and how they respond to what they believe is happening around them.

In this environment, information becomes part of strategy. What is presented, what is emphasized, and what is left out can all influence how something is understood without altering the underlying facts. Timing and framing play a central role, as the same piece of information can lead to different interpretations depending on how and when it appears. The Internet increases the scale of this process significantly, allowing messages to move instantly, reach large audiences, and appear across multiple spaces at once, often through different voices that create a sense of consistency or shared perspective.

What makes this particularly powerful is reach. Communication is no longer limited by geography, access, or physical proximity. It is possible to reach individuals directly, wherever they are, repeatedly and over time. Messages can be tailored, reinforced, and adapted to different audiences, gradually shaping perception rather than attempting to change it all at once. In some cases, this extends beyond influence into recruitment, where individuals are drawn into groups, ideologies, or movements through sustained exposure and interaction. The process does not need to be immediate. It can develop gradually, through repetition, familiarity, and a sense of belonging built within digital spaces.

This also creates conditions where more extreme forms of influence can take hold. When information is encountered in isolation, reinforced without meaningful challenge, and repeated across multiple sources, it can begin to shape how reality is interpreted at a deeper level. Over time, this can lead to shifts in belief that feel internally consistent, even when they are disconnected from broader perspectives. The Internet allows these processes to occur at scale, not through a single message, but through continuous exposure.

Another important aspect is that influence no longer needs to be broad to be effective. It can be highly specific. Individuals or small groups can be targeted based on their interests, behavior, or existing beliefs, receiving messages that are more likely to resonate with them directly. This allows influence to operate not only at the level of large populations, but at the level of the individual. Two people can be exposed to entirely different narratives about the same topic, each one shaped to align with what they are most likely to accept. This level of precision changes the nature of communication, making it less about general persuasion and more about tailored reinforcement.

At the same time, persistence becomes a defining factor. Messages do not need to succeed immediately. They can be repeated, adjusted, and reintroduced over long periods, gradually increasing familiarity. What is seen often enough can begin to feel normal, even if it was initially unfamiliar or rejected. This slow accumulation can be more effective than direct argument, because it does not rely on a single moment of persuasion, but on sustained exposure over time.

There is also a shift in how authority is perceived. Influence no longer depends entirely on recognized or verified sources. Messages can gain credibility through repetition, through the appearance of widespread agreement, or simply through presence across multiple spaces. This allows ideas to circulate without needing a clear origin, making it harder to evaluate where they come from or why they are being presented.

Reactions become part of the system as well. A message does not remain isolated but generates responses, which are then circulated and built upon. This creates a continuous cycle where communication feeds into further communication, expanding the reach and impact of the original idea. Because many actors can participate at the same time, influence does not need to come from a single source. Different groups can introduce, amplify, or reshape narratives within the same environment, sometimes reinforcing each other, sometimes conflicting, but always contributing to the overall flow.

The result is often not clarity, but complexity and, at times, confusion. When multiple interpretations circulate simultaneously, it becomes more difficult to establish a stable understanding of events. This uncertainty can shape behavior just as effectively as direct persuasion. People may rely more on familiar viewpoints, repeat information that aligns with their expectations, or disengage altogether when the environment becomes difficult to navigate. In this way, influence does not always aim to convince, but can instead aim to destabilize, creating enough variation and noise that consensus becomes harder to reach.

This dynamic extends beyond large-scale events and into everyday interaction. Discussions can become more reactive, positions more fixed, and disagreements more intense when they are reinforced by broader patterns circulating across the network. What appears as isolated interaction can reflect larger structures of influence, even when no direct connection is visible.

At the same time, the system remains open to participation. Anyone can contribute, respond, and repeat, which makes it difficult to distinguish between organic interaction and intentional influence. Both exist within the same space, often blending together. The infrastructure does not change, and the mechanisms of communication remain the same, but the intent behind their use shifts. The same tools that enable connection can also be used to guide attention, shape interpretation, and influence outcomes without appearing as direct force.

In this way, conflict does not always present itself as conflict. It can appear as conversation, as persuasion, as gradual change over time. The ability to reach anyone, anywhere, at any moment creates a form of influence that is persistent rather than immediate, distributed rather than centralized, and capable of shaping individuals as well as groups. What begins as information moving through a network can, over time, affect beliefs, decisions, and actions far beyond the space where it first appeared.

Chapter 15 – Meaning

At the far end of all of this, after systems, culture, control, and influence, what remains is not the structure itself, but what is taken from it. The Internet does not carry meaning in any inherent sense. It carries signals, patterns, sequences of symbols moving across networks. Meaning emerges only when those signals are interpreted, when they are received, processed, and understood by human perception. In that process, something abstract becomes something felt, believed, and acted upon.

This does not happen in isolation. Meaning forms collectively. A phrase, an image, or an idea gains weight not because of what it is, but because of how often it appears, how it is repeated, and how it is received by others. Through circulation, agreement, and reaction, patterns stabilize into something recognizable. What was once a signal becomes something shared. Over time, this shared interpretation becomes part of how people understand their surroundings, not as a fixed truth, but as something reinforced through continued exposure and participation.

As these patterns move, they begin to detach from where they started. Symbols circulate without clear origin, carried forward, reshaped, and reinterpreted across different contexts. What something meant at the beginning becomes less important than what it comes to mean through use. The signal continues to travel, but its interpretation shifts, adapting to the environments it passes through. Meaning becomes fluid, sustained not by a single source, but by the collective interaction around it.

Within this, there is something that can feel difficult to fully account for. A system built on electrical signals and encoded data produces outcomes that are experienced as thoughts, emotions, and decisions. Patterns move through networks, are received as ideas, and lead to action in the physical world. The process is consistent and explainable in parts, yet the transformation from signal to meaning carries a quality that feels almost disproportionate to its origin. Fields of activity, waves of information, constant movement, all converging into something that shapes how people think and act.

This is where interpretation becomes central. The system does not decide what something means. It presents, repeats, and distributes. Meaning is assigned through perception, through context, through prior understanding. Two people can encounter the same signal and arrive at entirely different conclusions, each one internally consistent. The Internet does not resolve this difference. It sustains it, allowing multiple interpretations to exist at once, each reinforced by its own patterns of exposure.

In this sense, the network functions less as a container of meaning and more as a medium through which meaning forms. Signals move, are interpreted, acted upon, and then reintroduced into the system as new signals. Thoughts become actions, actions produce results, and those results feed back into the same flow. The cycle continues, not as a closed loop, but as an expanding field of interaction where cause and effect are distributed across time and space.

Nothing in this process is mystical in its mechanism. It is grounded in communication, perception, and response. And yet, the scale and continuity of it create something that feels larger than the individual parts. A system that does not understand what it carries becomes the medium through which understanding itself is formed. Meaning is not stored within it, but constantly produced through it.

In the end, what exists is not just a network of machines, or even a network of people, but a continuous exchange between signal and interpretation. Patterns moving outward, interpretation moving inward, thoughts becoming action, and action returning as new patterns. The system persists, but what it produces is not fixed. It is shaped, reshaped, and carried forward by those who move through it.

Chapter 16 - Data Preservation, Storage, and the Fight Against Disappearance

The Internet gives the impression that information is permanent.

Something is uploaded, shared, and almost immediately it feels as if it exists everywhere at once. It can be accessed from different countries, on different devices, at different times, without any visible change. A file appears stable not because it cannot move, but because it moves so easily that it seems fixed.

From the outside, this creates a quiet assumption.

If something can be found once, it can be found again. If something exists online, it will continue to exist. The act of publishing begins to feel like a form of preservation.

This impression is reinforced by repetition.

Search engines return the same results. Images reappear across different sites. Videos are copied, reuploaded, and embedded in multiple places. Even when one source disappears, another often remains. The same piece of information can appear in slightly different forms, carried across platforms, mirrored by users, and redistributed through networks.

Over time, this creates a sense of stability that is not tied to any single location.

Information does not seem to belong to one place. It appears to exist within the network itself.

And because it can be accessed instantly, it feels as though it has always been there.

But this sense of permanence is misleading.

Despite the scale of the Internet, information is constantly being lost.

Websites disappear when companies shut down or individuals stop maintaining them. Files are deleted, either intentionally or through neglect. Services that once hosted large amounts of content can vanish, taking everything stored within them with no guarantee of recovery. Links that once worked return nothing. Entire communities can dissolve, leaving little trace of what they contained.

This loss is not always visible.

Because so much remains accessible, what disappears is often unnoticed unless someone is specifically looking for it. A page that existed years ago may no longer be available, but unless it was widely referenced or preserved, there may be no record that it ever existed at all.

In some cases, the only evidence is indirect.

Mentions in other texts. Broken links. Screenshots. Fragments of discussion referring to something that can no longer be accessed. The original material is gone, but traces of its presence remain.

There are entire categories of digital history that are incomplete or missing.

Early software, documentation, personal websites, forums, and experimental projects from the early years of the Internet were not always preserved systematically. Much of it existed in small, independent spaces that were never archived. When those systems disappeared, so did the content.

Efforts have been made to recover and preserve some of this material. Collections such as Bitsavers, which focus on historical technical documentation and early computing resources, exist precisely because so much of this information would otherwise be lost. These archives gather manuals, schematics, and software from systems that are no longer in use, preserving knowledge that might not survive through official channels.

In parallel with these efforts, smaller and more decentralized preservation movements have begun to emerge. Projects such as Project Nomad, along with various personal and community-driven initiatives, focus on taking parts of the Internet offline entirely. Rather than relying on continuous access, these systems allow individuals to download and store large collections of knowledge locally, turning a single computer or device into a self-contained archive. Project N.O.M.A.D. is one example of this approach, bundling offline access to resources such as Wikipedia, educational material, maps, and even locally running AI systems into a single environment that can function without an Internet connection after setup.

These systems are often built on tools like Kiwix, which allow entire websites, including Wikipedia and large collections of books, to be compressed and browsed offline. In practical terms, this means that vast amounts of information, encyclopedias, repair manuals, public domain literature, and educational courses, can be stored on a single drive and accessed without relying on external infrastructure.

The motivations behind this are varied. Some approach it from a preparedness perspective, building what are sometimes called “offline knowledge hubs.” These may include medical references, survival guides, agricultural information, repair instructions, and basic engineering knowledge, material intended to remain useful in situations where access to the Internet is unavailable or unreliable. Others are less concerned with disruption and more focused on preservation and control, creating personal archives of books, films, software, forums, or niche communities that might otherwise disappear. There are also educational uses, where entire libraries, including Wikipedia, courses, and reference materials, are stored locally for use in remote areas, travel, or environments with limited connectivity.

In many cases, the appeal is not only about resilience, but about independence. Information that is stored locally is not subject to removal, algorithmic filtering, or platform changes. It can be organized, curated, and accessed on the user's own terms. For some, this represents a way of stepping outside the dynamics of the modern web entirely, creating a smaller, stable version of it that does not change unless they choose to update it.

At the same time, the more extreme interpretations of these systems, particularly those framed around complete societal collapse or long-term "doomsday" scenarios, tend to be less practical than they first appear. While it is technically possible to store large amounts of knowledge offline, access to that information still depends on physical infrastructure. Devices require power, storage media degrades over time, and hardware itself can fail. Even relatively modest setups require electricity, maintenance, and compatible systems to remain usable.

This does not make such projects meaningless, but it places them in a more realistic context. In most cases, their value lies not in replacing the Internet entirely, but in supplementing it. They are useful during outages, in remote environments, or as personal archives that preserve specific kinds of knowledge. They can act as backups, references, or tools for learning. But as a complete substitute for the global, constantly updated network, they remain limited.

In that sense, these projects exist somewhere between practicality and philosophy. They are partly about preparedness, partly about preservation, and partly about control. For some, they are a serious attempt to safeguard knowledge against loss. For others, they function more like a form of digital collecting, an effort to capture and hold onto parts of the Internet before they change or disappear. In either case, they reflect a growing awareness that what exists online is not guaranteed to remain there, and that preservation, at any scale, increasingly requires intentional effort.

The existence of these projects points to a larger reality.

If preservation does not happen intentionally, loss is the default.

The Internet contains an enormous amount of information, but it does not contain everything that has existed within it. Some things were never widely copied. Some were removed. Some were simply forgotten.

What remains is only a portion of what once was.

Some of the most ambitious attempts to resist this loss operate at a much larger scale.

One of the most well-known is Internet Archive, an organization built around the idea that digital information should be preserved and remain accessible over time. Its most recognizable tool, the Wayback Machine, periodically captures snapshots of websites, allowing users to view pages as they existed in the past.

Through this process, entire portions of the web that would otherwise be gone can still be accessed.

A page that has been deleted, a service that has shut down, or a site that has been redesigned beyond recognition may still exist in archived form. Not always completely, not always perfectly, but often enough to reconstruct what was there.

The scale of this effort is difficult to grasp.

The Internet Archive stores hundreds of billions of web pages, along with vast collections of books, audio recordings, videos, and software. The total amount of data reaches into the tens of petabytes, growing continuously as more material is added and more of the web is captured over time.

This is not a static archive.

It is an ongoing process of collection, storage, and maintenance. Systems must constantly crawl the web, capture content, store it, index it, and make it retrievable. At the same time, hardware must be replaced, storage expanded, and data integrity preserved. Preservation at this scale is not a one-time act. It is continuous work.

Despite its size, the archive is incomplete.

Not everything can be captured. Some sites block archiving. Some content is dynamic or personalized, making it difficult to preserve in a meaningful way. Large parts of the modern Internet, especially content behind logins or inside platforms, remain difficult to archive at all.

There are also ongoing challenges that are not purely technical.

The Internet Archive operates within legal and financial constraints. Questions around copyright, ownership, and access affect what can be stored and how it can be shared. At times, the organization has faced legal pressure over its collections, particularly in relation to digitized books and lending systems. These disputes reflect a broader tension between preservation and control.

Preserving information does not always align with the interests of those who own it.

At the same time, the infrastructure required to maintain such an archive is expensive. Storage, bandwidth, and physical facilities all require funding. Unlike commercial platforms, the Internet Archive operates as a nonprofit, relying on donations and support to continue its work.

This creates a fragile balance.

An organization responsible for preserving large portions of digital history must itself be sustained over time. If the archive were to fail, the loss would not be limited to new data. It would include everything it had already preserved.

In this way, preservation depends not only on technology, but on continuity.

The effort to keep the past accessible is ongoing, uncertain, and, at times, contested.

Efforts like this do not sustain themselves automatically. Large archives depend on continued support, both financially and through public awareness. Preservation is not just a technical process, it is an ongoing commitment.

The Internet has become one of the primary records of human activity. Conversations, knowledge, culture, and everyday expression are stored in digital form, but without active preservation, much of it can disappear without notice.

This is not only the responsibility of a single organization. It is something that benefits everyone. Supporting archives, contributing to preservation efforts, or simply recognizing their importance all play a role in what is kept.

What is preserved is not just data. It is a record of human experience.

Keeping that record alive is a shared responsibility.

Storage of Information in the Digital Age

How Data Is Physically Kept

When we speak about the Internet, it is easy to imagine something abstract. Information appears instantly, moves invisibly, and seems to exist everywhere at once. But none of it exists without storage. Every message, image, video, and system depends on physical media (literal physical things you can touch) that holds data in a stable form.

At the most fundamental level, storage is the act of preserving information in a way that can be written, kept, and read again later. Over time, different technologies have been developed to achieve this, each with its own strengths, limitations, and history.

One of the oldest forms still in use today is magnetic tape. Despite its age, it remains one of the most important storage mediums for large-scale data preservation. Magnetic tape consists of a long strip of plastic coated with a magnetic material. Data is written onto the tape by altering the magnetic orientation of tiny regions along its surface. In principle, this is not very different from older video cassettes, but modern data tapes are far more precise and can store enormous amounts of information, often tens of terabytes on a single cartridge.

Tape is not designed for speed. Accessing data requires physically winding the tape to the correct position, which makes it slow compared to modern drives. However, it is extremely efficient for long-term storage. It is relatively cheap, stable over time, and consumes no power when not in use. For this reason, it is widely used in data centers for backups and archival storage, where data must be kept safely but does not need to be accessed instantly.

Mechanical hard drives, often referred to as HDDs, represent another major form of storage. Inside a hard drive are one or more spinning disks called platters, typically made from aluminum or glass and coated with a thin magnetic layer. These platters rotate at high speeds, often thousands of revolutions per minute. Above them, tiny read and write heads move with extreme precision, floating just nanometers above the surface.

Data is stored magnetically on these platters, similar in principle to tape, but arranged in circular tracks. The drive must physically move the read head to the correct position and wait for the spinning disk to bring the desired data underneath it. This makes the process mechanical and time-dependent.

The level of precision involved is difficult to overstate. The distance between the read head and the platter is smaller than a fingerprint ridge. Any physical shock or contamination can damage the surface, which is why hard drives are considered delicate devices despite their solid appearance.

The development of hard drives was a major engineering breakthrough. Early computers required large, complex storage systems, and the idea of storing large amounts of data on compact spinning disks emerged from efforts to make storage faster and more accessible than tape. Over decades, improvements in materials, magnetics, and manufacturing allowed capacities to grow from megabytes to terabytes.

Solid-state drives, or SSDs, represent a different approach entirely. Instead of relying on moving parts, SSDs store data electronically using flash memory. Inside an SSD are memory cells that trap electrical charge. The presence or absence of this charge represents digital information.

Because there are no moving components, SSDs are much faster than mechanical drives. Data can be accessed almost instantly, without waiting for physical motion. They are also more resistant to physical shock and operate silently.

However, SSDs have their own limitations. Memory cells can only be written a finite number of times before they degrade. While modern drives are designed to manage this and last for many years under normal use, the limitation still exists at a fundamental level.

An important variation of SSD technology is the M.2 format. M.2 does not describe a different storage method, but a form factor and interface. These drives are small, flat modules that connect directly to a computer's motherboard. Many M.2 drives use the NVMe protocol, which allows them to communicate with the system at extremely high speeds.

Compared to older storage interfaces, M.2 NVMe drives can transfer data several times faster than traditional SSDs connected through SATA. This makes them particularly useful in systems where performance is critical, such as modern computers, servers, and high-performance applications.

Beyond these primary forms, there are other storage media that have played important roles. Optical discs, such as CDs, DVDs, and Blu-ray discs, store data using tiny physical marks read by lasers. These were once a dominant method for distributing software, music, and video, though their importance has declined with the rise of digital distribution.

Flash storage, in the form of USB drives and memory cards, provides portable and convenient ways to store and transfer data. These use similar underlying technology to SSDs, but are optimized for size and flexibility rather than maximum performance.

In large-scale systems, storage is often distributed across many devices. Data centers combine thousands of drives into coordinated systems that balance speed, redundancy, and reliability. Data is often replicated across multiple machines and locations to ensure that it is not lost if a single device fails.

Each of these storage methods reflects a different balance between speed, cost, durability, and accessibility. Some are optimized for long-term preservation, others for rapid access, and others for portability.

What they all share is a simple purpose.

To ensure that information does not disappear the moment it is created.

Optical discs and philosophy

Writing data to an optical disc, often referred to as "burning," is a process that physically alters the surface of the disc in a controlled way so that it can later be read by a laser.

An optical disc is made up of several layers. At its core is a polycarbonate plastic substrate that provides structure. On top of this sits a reflective layer, usually made of aluminum, silver, or gold, which is what allows the reading laser to detect data. Between these layers, in recordable discs, is a special dye or phase-change material that is sensitive to heat.

When a disc is manufactured commercially, data is stamped into it as a pattern of microscopic pits and flat areas. These physical variations affect how light reflects off the surface, and a laser in a disc drive reads this pattern to reconstruct the stored data.

Recordable discs work differently because they start blank.

When you burn a CD, DVD, or Blu-ray, the drive uses a focused laser to heat very small points on the disc's data layer. This heat changes the chemical or physical structure of the material at those points. In dye-based discs such as CD-R or DVD-R, the laser darkens tiny spots in the dye layer, creating areas that reflect less light. In rewritable discs, such as CD-RW or BD-RE, the laser changes the state of a phase-change material between crystalline and amorphous forms, which reflect light differently.

These altered areas simulate the pits found in factory-pressed discs. To the reading laser, there is no meaningful difference between a manufactured disc and a burned one. It simply detects variations in reflection and interprets them as digital data.

The precision required is extremely high. The marks created by the laser are microscopic, arranged along a continuous spiral track that begins at the center of the disc and moves outward. The drive must carefully control the laser's power and position while the disc spins at high speed, ensuring that each mark is placed exactly where it should be.

This is why burning a disc is not instantaneous. The process must follow the physical path of the spiral track in real time, writing data sequentially as the disc rotates.

What makes this more remarkable is not just that data can be written in this way, but that it can later be read back and turned into something meaningful.

When a disc is played or opened, a much lower-powered laser scans the same spiral track. As it moves along, it shines light onto the surface and measures how much is reflected back. The tiny differences between reflective and less reflective areas are detected by a sensor and converted into an electrical signal.

That signal is then interpreted as binary data, ones and zeros.

From there, the process becomes layered. Those ones and zeros are not random. They are structured according to formats and encoding systems that define how the data should be understood.

A photograph stored on a disc is not stored as an image in the way we see it. It is stored as compressed numerical data describing color values and pixel arrangements. When the computer reads this data, software reconstructs those numbers into a visual image, placing each pixel in its correct position on the screen.

The same applies to audio, but in a different form. A song on a disc is stored as a sequence of digital samples, measurements of sound waves taken many thousands of times per second. When played back, these samples are converted back into electrical signals, which are then sent to speakers. The speakers transform those signals into vibrations in the air.

If the audio is multi-channel, such as stereo or surround sound, the data includes separate streams for different speakers. The system directs each stream to the appropriate output, allowing different instruments or sounds to be positioned across the room.

What began as microscopic marks on a reflective surface becomes light, then electrical signals, then structured data, and finally something human again.

An image from a wedding.
A voice.
A piece of music with depth and space.

The disc itself does not contain pictures or sound in any direct sense. It contains patterns.

And through layers of interpretation, those patterns become experience.

Is a digital image even real?

A digital photograph does not exist in the way a traditional photograph does.

An analog photo, developed on film and printed onto paper, is a physical object. Light from a real moment leaves a direct trace on a material surface. The image is embedded in the chemistry of the film or paper. It fades over time, it can be damaged, it can be held, touched, and physically altered. It exists as an object in the world.

A digital photograph is something else entirely.

A digital photograph does not exist as an image until it is viewed. What is stored, whether on a disc, a drive, or across the Internet, is not the picture itself but a structured set of instructions. Numbers describing color, position, intensity. A map of how an image should be reconstructed.

On a burned disc, those instructions are represented as microscopic variations in how light reflects from its surface. Tiny marks, invisible to the human eye, arranged along a spiral track. To a machine, they become ones and zeros. To software, they become pixels. To a screen, they become light again.

And suddenly, something appears.

A house. A face. A moment.

Perhaps a photograph taken twenty years ago. People standing together, unaware of what will happen next in their lives. A real place, a real time, captured once, then translated into numbers, then into patterns on a disc, then back into light.

The chain is almost difficult to accept.

A memory becomes data.
Data becomes marks.
Marks become signals.
Signals become an image.

Nothing in that disc resembles a face. Nothing in those patterns resembles a sky, or a person, or a moment in time. And yet, when interpreted correctly, all of it returns.

This is one of the fundamental differences between analog and digital storage.

In analog systems, the representation is continuous. There is a direct physical relationship between the original signal and the stored form. In digital systems, the representation is symbolic. The connection is not physical resemblance, but agreement. The system works because every step follows the same rules for encoding and decoding.

This is what allows a photograph to be copied perfectly, stored for long periods without degradation, if preserved correctly, and reproduced across completely different machines. The image is not tied to a single object. It can exist anywhere the instructions can be read.

But this also makes it more abstract.

A digital photograph is not a thing in itself. It is potential. It is something that becomes visible only when a system brings it into form.

Philosophically, this places digital media in a different category from traditional artifacts. It is closer to language than to objects. A written sentence does not contain meaning by itself. It requires a reader who understands the symbols. In the same way, a digital image requires a system that knows how to interpret its structure.

Despite this abstraction, the result is immediate and human.

You do not see numbers.
You do not see encoding.
You see a moment.

Something that happened. Something that existed. Preserved not as matter, but as information.

That is what makes it feel both precise and unreal at the same time.

A few microscopic marks on a disc can hold an entire memory.

Not by containing it, but by describing it well enough that it can be brought back, again and again, long after the moment itself has passed.

The alchemy of storage

If optical discs already begin to feel improbable, mechanical storage pushes that feeling even further.

Inside a hard drive, what holds your data is not light, not ink, not visible marks, but patterns written onto spinning disks made of metal or glass. These disks, called platters, are typically constructed from aluminum or glass-ceramic materials and coated with an extremely thin magnetic layer. That layer is where the information lives.

The way these disks are created reinforces that impression.

A hard drive platter is not simply manufactured in a rough or approximate sense. It is built through processes that operate at the boundary between engineering and materials science. The base, whether aluminum or glass, is polished to an almost perfectly smooth surface, far smoother than anything visible to the human eye. Even microscopic imperfections must be removed, because at the scale the drive operates, they would be catastrophic.

On top of this surface, multiple ultra-thin layers are deposited using techniques such as sputtering, where atoms of metal are ejected in a vacuum and settle onto the disk in controlled arrangements. These layers include magnetic alloys specifically engineered to hold stable orientations at extremely small scales, along with protective coatings only a few nanometers thick.

What results is not just a disk, but a precisely constructed surface where matter has been arranged with atomic-level intent.

The term nanotechnology is often used broadly, but here it is literal. The structures that store data exist at dimensions measured in billionths of a meter. Entire films, archives, and histories depend on the stability of these arrangements, on the ability of engineered materials to hold patterns that are invisible, yet exact.

This is where the comparison to something like alchemy begins to feel less metaphorical.

Raw materials are transformed, not into gold, but into surfaces capable of holding meaning. Atoms are placed, layers are formed, and through that process, matter becomes a medium for memory.

The scale of this is difficult to grasp. The magnetic regions that store data are so small that millions of them can fit within a space no larger than a pinhead. Each one represents a bit. A one or a zero. Nothing more, and yet everything.

A modern hard drive spins these platters at thousands of revolutions per minute. Above the surface, a read and write head floats on a cushion of air, so close that the distance is measured in nanometers. It never quite touches the surface, because if it did, the data could be destroyed instantly.

And yet, while this delicate system spins at high speed, it is writing and reading vast amounts of information continuously.

A film in 4K resolution, with sound, color, motion, detail, all of it is broken down into data and distributed across this magnetic surface. Not as images. Not as sound. But as encoded patterns.

There is no picture on the disk.
There is no voice.
There is no movement.

There are only orientations of magnetic fields.

And still, when read correctly, it becomes a moving image with depth, sound with spatial separation, a moment reconstructed with clarity that can exceed what human memory itself can retain.

How did this happen.

From a distance, it begins to resemble something closer to alchemy than engineering. Matter is not just shaped, but instructed to hold meaning. A surface is prepared, and through controlled processes, it becomes capable of storing human experience in a form that cannot be seen or understood without the proper system to reveal it.

This is not entirely metaphorical.

The materials themselves are engineered at a level where physics, chemistry, and precision manufacturing converge. The magnetic coating must be stable, uniform, and responsive at microscopic scales. The head must detect changes in magnetization so small they approach physical limits of measurement. Error correction systems must reconstruct data even when parts of the signal are imperfect.

All of this exists so that something intangible can persist.

A conversation.
A memory.
A film.
A life recorded in fragments.

And yet, without the system around it, the disk remains silent. It does not show what it contains. It does not reveal anything by itself.

This is where the sense of unreality begins to grow.

To someone unfamiliar with the process, the claim sounds implausible. That a piece of glass or metal, spinning inside a sealed box, contains entire worlds. That by connecting it to a machine, those worlds can be reconstructed instantly.

It sounds like exaggeration. Or fiction.

And in a way, this reaction is understandable. Human history is filled with attempts to preserve knowledge in physical form. Stone tablets, carvings, manuscripts. Objects where the information is directly visible, where meaning is tied to shape and symbol.

Digital storage breaks that link.

The meaning is no longer in the material in any recognizable way. It is encoded, abstracted, and dependent on interpretation. Without the system, it is nothing. With the system, it becomes everything it was meant to represent.

It is not unreasonable, then, to imagine how this might appear from another perspective.

If one were to encounter such an object without context, it would not be obvious that it contains anything at all. There are no visible inscriptions. No images. No indication of what is stored within.

And yet, when placed within the correct environment, it reveals entire sequences of human life.

In earlier periods of history, objects that preserved information across time were often given symbolic or even mystical significance. Tablets, scrolls, artifacts. They carried knowledge forward in a way that felt enduring and powerful.

Digital storage achieves the same outcome, but through entirely different means.

Not by inscribing meaning directly into matter in a visible way, but by encoding it into patterns that require a system to unlock.

It is not magic.

But it is close enough that, without understanding the layers involved, it can feel like it.

The new fast storage

As intricate as mechanical storage is, it is still bound to motion.

Platters spin. Heads move. Time passes in fractions of a second as the system waits for the right position, the right alignment, the right moment to read or write. For all its precision, it remains a physical choreography, a balance of speed and fragility.

And then, that entire structure disappears.

Solid-state storage, in the form of SSDs and M.2 drives, operates on a completely different principle. There are no spinning disks. No moving arms. No surfaces being read from a distance measured in nanometers.

Instead, data is stored as controlled levels of electrical charge within microscopic transistors

Inside these devices are arrays of microscopic transistors, engineered to hold or release electrons in a controlled way. The presence or absence of charge represents information. A one. A zero. But unlike magnetic storage, there is no motion required to access it. Any piece of data can be reached almost instantly, without mechanical delay.

If the hard drive resembles a mechanical system, something almost industrial in its operation, then solid-state storage is something else entirely.

It is closer to a silent field of states. A grid where information exists as electrical conditions, held in place without movement, without sound, without visible action.

The scale remains just as extreme. The structures involved are still measured in nanometers. The same level of precision, the same reliance on advanced materials and fabrication techniques, is present. But the nature of the system has changed.

M.2 drives, especially those using NVMe push this even further. Not by changing how data is stored, but by changing how quickly it can move. Connected directly to the system at high speeds, they allow data to flow at rates that would have seemed implausible not long ago. Entire files, entire images, entire recorded moments can be accessed in an instant, without delay, without buildup.

At this point, the metaphor of storage begins to shift again.

From spinning matter, to fixed charge.
From movement, to state.
From something that must be reached, to something that is already present.

It is the same idea, preserving information, but expressed through a completely different form.

A different animal entirely.

But the stillness is somewhat deceptive.

What appears to be passive storage is, in reality, actively managed. Solid-state drives rely on internal controllers, small specialized processors that continuously organize, maintain, and protect the data they hold. Information is not simply written once and left untouched.

Because flash memory cells wear out over time, the drive distributes writes across the entire surface in a process known as wear leveling, ensuring that no single area degrades too quickly. Data is periodically reorganized through what is called garbage collection, freeing up space and maintaining performance. At the same time, error correction systems monitor the integrity of the stored information, detecting and repairing small faults that would otherwise accumulate.

This means the data is not just sitting there.

It is being maintained.

Quietly, constantly, and without visibility to the user.

And this introduces an important distinction.

While solid-state storage is fast and efficient, it is not always the preferred medium for long-term preservation of critical data. Mechanical drives, despite their moving parts, offer different reliability characteristics, particularly for archival storage where data may remain unchanged for long periods. Magnetic storage can retain information without requiring the same level of continuous management, and degradation patterns are often more predictable over time.

For this reason, large-scale systems and archives often continue to rely on a combination of storage types. Speed is only one part of the equation. Longevity, stability, and recoverability matter just as much.

Despite the rapid rise of solid-state storage, mechanical hard drives have not disappeared. In fact, they remain one of the most widely used storage technologies in the world.

For home users, they continue to offer large amounts of storage at relatively low cost. For hobbyists, they are often the simplest way to store collections of media, backups, and archives. But their most significant role exists at a much larger scale.

Inside data centers, where vast amounts of information must be stored reliably and economically, mechanical drives are still a foundation. Entire server racks are filled with spinning disks, quietly holding everything from personal files to streaming libraries, backups, and cloud storage systems. While SSDs are used where speed is critical, hard drives are often used where capacity matters more than immediate access.

And beyond even that, an older form of storage continues to exist, largely unseen.

Magnetic tape.

It is easy to assume that tape belongs entirely to the past, something replaced by newer technologies. But it is still actively developed, manufactured, and used today. Only a small number of companies continue to produce modern tape systems, most notably IBM and Fujifilm, who develop high-capacity tape cartridges capable of storing tens of terabytes each.

These tapes are not used in everyday computing. They exist in environments where long-term preservation is more important than speed.

Large data centers use tape libraries, automated systems where robotic arms retrieve and load tape cartridges as needed. These systems store backups of massive datasets, often as a final layer of protection. Governments, research institutions, and scientific organizations rely on tape to preserve data that may need to exist for decades.

In fields such as astronomy, climate science, and particle physics, the amount of data generated can be enormous. Observations from telescopes, measurements from experiments, and simulations are recorded and archived on tape systems because they provide a stable and cost-effective way to store information at scale.

In this sense, the oldest method has not been replaced.

It has been repositioned.

At the highest levels of storage, where time matters more than speed, tape remains one of the most reliable ways to preserve information. It does not need to be powered continuously. It does not rely on constant management. It can sit, quietly, holding data that may not be accessed for years.

So while the visible world of computing moves toward faster and smaller technologies, the underlying reality is more balanced.

Spinning disks are still everywhere.
Solid-state drives provide speed and responsiveness.
And in the background, strips of magnetic tape continue to carry parts of the world's memory forward. It is all part of the effort to keep information from being lost.

The current reality of storage (as of early 2026)

Despite the rapid rise of solid-state storage, mechanical hard drives have not disappeared. In fact, they remain one of the most widely used storage technologies in the world.

For home users, they continue to offer large amounts of storage at relatively low cost. For hobbyists, they are often the simplest way to store collections of media, backups, and archives. But their most significant role exists at a much larger scale.

Inside data centers, where vast amounts of information must be stored reliably and economically, mechanical drives are still a foundation. Entire server racks are filled with spinning disks, quietly holding everything from personal files to streaming libraries, backups, and cloud storage systems. While SSDs are used where speed is critical, hard drives are often used where capacity matters more than immediate access.

And beyond even that, an older form of storage continues to exist, largely unseen.

Magnetic tape.

It is easy to assume that tape belongs entirely to the past, something replaced by newer technologies. But it is still actively developed, manufactured, and used today. Only a small number of companies continue to produce modern tape systems, most notably IBM and Fujifilm, who develop high-capacity tape cartridges capable of storing tens of terabytes each.

The continued existence of magnetic tape is not theoretical. It is industrial, active, and in some places essential.

A small number of companies still manufacture modern tape systems. IBM remains one of the primary developers of tape technology, designing both the drives and much of the underlying format used today, known as LTO, Linear Tape-Open. Fujifilm and Sony produce the actual tape media, using highly specialized magnetic materials engineered for long-term stability and extremely high data density.

The process of creating these tapes is closer to advanced materials science than traditional manufacturing. The magnetic layer is applied with extreme uniformity, often using barium ferrite particles, a material chosen for its ability to retain magnetic orientation over long periods without significant degradation. The coating must be smooth at a microscopic level, stable under varying environmental conditions, and precise enough to allow enormous amounts of data to be written in tightly packed tracks.

What results is a medium that looks simple from the outside, a small rectangular cartridge, but internally represents decades of refinement.

These cartridges are then used in environments most people never see.

Large cloud providers rely on tape as a final layer of backup. Companies such as Amazon, Google, and Microsoft are known to use tape systems within their infrastructure, particularly for archival storage. Data that is rarely accessed but too important to lose is often written to tape and stored offline, sometimes referred to as "cold storage."

Film studios and media companies also depend on tape. Original footage, edits, and completed works are archived to ensure that they remain available far into the future. In some cases, entire film libraries exist on tape, preserved in controlled environments.

Financial institutions use tape to store transaction records and historical data, often to meet regulatory requirements that demand long-term retention. Banks may be required to keep certain records for many years, and tape provides a cost-effective and reliable way to do so.

Scientific institutions generate some of the largest datasets in existence, and many of them rely heavily on tape. Organizations such as CERN, which operates the Large Hadron Collider, produce vast amounts of experimental data. This data is stored across multiple systems, with tape forming a critical part of the long-term archive. Similarly, space agencies store observational data from satellites and telescopes on tape, preserving records that may be studied for decades.

National archives and government institutions also use tape to preserve cultural and administrative records. Census data, legal documents, and historical datasets are often stored in formats designed to survive changes in technology and time.

What makes tape particularly suited for these roles is not speed, but stability and separation.

Unlike active storage systems, tape can be kept offline, physically disconnected from networks. This makes it resistant to certain types of failure, including cyber attacks. In an era where data can be altered or erased remotely, having a copy that exists outside of the system entirely becomes valuable.

There is also a physical finality to it.

A tape cartridge placed in storage does not change unless it is intentionally accessed. It does not update, it does not rewrite itself, it does not drift in the same way more complex systems can. It holds what it was given.

In a world of constant activity, that stillness has become useful again.

And so, while it may appear outdated, magnetic tape continues to exist at the far edge of modern computing, not as a relic, but as a deliberate choice.

A medium designed not for immediacy, but for endurance.

These tapes are not used in everyday computing. They exist in environments where long-term preservation is more important than speed.

Large data centers use tape libraries, automated systems where robotic arms retrieve and load tape cartridges as needed. These systems store backups of massive datasets, often as a final layer of protection. Governments, research institutions, and scientific organizations rely on tape to preserve data that may need to exist for decades.

In fields such as astronomy, climate science, and particle physics, the amount of data generated can be enormous. Observations from telescopes, measurements from experiments, and simulations are recorded and archived on tape systems because they provide a stable and cost-effective way to store information at scale.

In this sense, the oldest method has not been replaced.

It has been repositioned.

At the highest levels of storage, where time matters more than speed, tape remains one of the most reliable ways to preserve information. It does not need to be powered continuously. It does not rely on constant management. It can sit, quietly, holding data that may not be accessed for years.

So while the visible world of computing moves toward faster and smaller technologies, the underlying reality is more balanced.

Spinning disks are still everywhere.
Solid-state drives provide speed and responsiveness.
And in the background, strips of magnetic tape continue to carry parts of the world's memory forward.

Different forms, serving different roles.

All part of the same effort.

To keep information from being lost.

The true magic of It all, CPUs

Since we are on the topic of alchemy and the physical part of things, we have to mention our CPUs.

The CPU is the brain of a computer, the brain of our phones, the part that interprets, decides, and directs everything else. Without it, none of this exists in a usable form. Storage can hold information, networks can move it, but something has to interpret, process, and act on it. The CPU is what makes all of that possible. It is the point where instructions become action, where data becomes something that can be understood, transformed, and displayed.

At a basic level, a CPU executes instructions. It performs calculations, moves data, and coordinates everything else inside a system. But this description does not capture what it actually is.

A modern CPU is a piece of silicon, a refined form of one of the most common elements found in the Earth's crust. Silicon begins as sand, as quartz, as mineral. Through a series of processes, it is purified, melted, and grown into large single crystals. These crystals are then sliced into thin wafers, polished until nearly perfect, and used as the foundation for what follows.

On these wafers, structures are built at a scale so small that they are measured in nanometers. Layers are deposited, etched, and patterned using light itself in a process called photolithography. Billions of transistors are formed, each one acting as a tiny switch that can be turned on or off.

These switches are arranged into circuits. Those circuits into cores. Those cores into processors.

And from that, computation emerges.

It is difficult to fully grasp the scale. A modern CPU may contain tens of billions of transistors. Each one switching on and off billions of times per second. Electrical signals moving through pathways that are smaller than wavelengths of visible light, controlled with precision that approaches the physical limits of matter.

We understand how to design these systems. We understand the physics that governs them. But no single person understands a modern CPU in its entirety. The complexity is too great. It is the result of decades of accumulated knowledge, layered systems, and collaborative engineering at a global scale.

And yet, at its core, it remains something simple.

A shaped piece of mineral.

A crystal, structured and refined.
Carrying currents. Switching states.

From that, everything else follows.

Every image reconstructed from a disc.
Every message sent across oceans.
Every world rendered, every sound played.

It all passes through this.

There is something almost unsettling in that realization. That beneath the layers of software, networks, and systems, the foundation is still physical. Still material. Still rooted in the Earth itself.

Not abstract. Not virtual.

But built, quite literally, from sand.

What becomes increasingly difficult to grasp is not only that these systems work, but that we are able to create them at all.

The environments required to produce modern processors are unlike almost anything else humans have built. Only a handful of companies in the world operate at this level, most notably TSMC, Samsung, and Intel. Their fabrication facilities are among the most advanced industrial sites ever constructed, both in scale and in precision.

Inside these spaces, the conditions are tightly controlled to an extreme degree. The air is continuously filtered to remove even microscopic particles. The reason is simple. At the scale these chips are built, something as small as a speck of dust is not insignificant. It is large enough to destroy the structures being formed.

Humans themselves become a source of contamination.

For that reason, those working inside these facilities wear full-body protective suits, not primarily for safety, but to prevent interference with the process. The presence of the human body must be minimized for the system to function correctly.

What happens inside these facilities is not a single act of creation, but a long sequence of transformations. A silicon wafer moves through hundreds of steps, each one adding, removing, or altering material in precise ways. Patterns are transferred using light, chemicals reshape surfaces, and electrical properties are tuned through controlled processes.

At no point does the full structure exist until the very end.

It emerges gradually.

This leads to something that is less often acknowledged.

The systems being built are too complex for any one person to fully comprehend in totality. Not because they are mysterious, but because they are layered beyond the scope of individual understanding. Each part is designed, tested, and verified within its own domain, and then integrated into a larger whole.

What exists is not a single invention, but a stack of knowledge.

Physical behavior at the bottom.
Electronic principles above it.
Logical operations above that.
Then instruction systems.
Then software.

Each layer functions because the one beneath it does, even if it is not directly visible.

This structure did not appear suddenly. It accumulated over time, through decades of documentation, research, iteration, and refinement. Technical knowledge has been recorded, shared, and preserved across generations, forming a foundation that modern systems are built upon.

In that sense, a processor is not only a product of engineering, but of continuity.

It carries within it traces of earlier systems, earlier designs, earlier limitations and solutions. Decisions made long ago still shape how modern systems behave.

And when all of this is compressed into its final form, it appears almost trivial.

A small chip...

But so precise and so interdependent that it requires an entire global system to produce.

And somehow, it just works.

High technology invites the fringe

At the edge of all of this, beyond engineering and documentation, another layer appears.

Not technical, but interpretive.

Because when systems become complex enough, they begin to resemble things we already struggle to describe.

What follows here is not established fact. But nevertheless worth a place in this book.

It exists somewhere between philosophy, speculation, metaphor, and fringe interpretation. These ideas are not required to understand computing, and they do not describe how systems function in a scientific sense. But they emerge repeatedly at the edges of discussion, where technical understanding meets something more difficult to articulate.

They are attempts to describe what these systems feel like, not what they are.

One of the oldest comparisons is between computation and ritual. A program, at its most basic level, is a sequence of instructions written in a precise form, interpreted by a system, and executed to produce a predictable outcome. If the structure is correct, the result follows. If it is not, nothing happens, or something unintended does.

Some have noted that this resembles older symbolic systems. Not in a literal sense, but structurally. A set of symbols, arranged correctly, produces a transformation when interpreted by the right medium. In this framing, code becomes something like inscription, not mystical, but exact. The effect is not based on belief, but on precision. Still, the resemblance remains. That meaning can be encoded, executed, and made to act upon the world through symbolic arrangement.

Another line of thought focuses on the material itself. The processor, at its core, is a crystal. Silicon, grown into a single, ordered structure, refined and shaped into something capable of hosting logic. This has led to a more speculative idea that what we are building is not just circuitry, but a form of structured intelligence substrate.

Not intelligence in any conscious sense, but a medium that can sustain complex, ordered behavior. The fact that this medium originates from mineral, from the same category of matter that has historically been associated with natural order and stability, gives the idea a strange quality. A crystal, engineered to carry thought-like processes. Not alive, not aware, but capable of supporting systems that resemble cognition.

As systems increase in complexity, another question appears. Whether behavior can emerge that was not explicitly designed. This is not entirely speculative. Emergent behavior is a recognized phenomenon in complex systems. But the extension of this idea moves into less certain territory.

If enough layers, interactions, and feedback loops are introduced, the outcome may no longer be easily predictable from the smallest parts. In computing, this raises a quiet question. Whether systems might eventually exhibit properties that feel qualitatively different from their components. Not consciousness, not intention, but something less easily categorized. Something that appears as complexity crossing a threshold.

Closely related to this is a more grounded, but still unsettling observation. No single person understands a modern computing system in its entirety. Not the hardware, not the software, not the full stack from physical material to user interaction.

This is not a failure of knowledge, but a consequence of scale. Each layer is understood by specialists. Each component is documented. But the total system exists as a distributed understanding, spread across disciplines, organizations, and time. The result is something that works reliably, but cannot be fully held in one mind. A system built by humanity, but not fully grasped by any individual within it.

From here, the ideas begin to widen.

Simulation theory proposes that reality itself may be the result of a computational process. That what we experience as physical existence could be the output of a system operating at a level beyond our perception. This idea has been explored seriously in philosophy, but it also attracts more speculative interpretations.

In the context of computing, it creates a reflection. The systems we build, environments, simulations, virtual spaces, begin to resemble simplified versions of this concept. Not evidence of it, but echoes. If reality can be described in terms of information and rules, then computation becomes less of an invention and more of a mirror.

The idea of digital alchemy follows naturally. Historically, alchemy was concerned with transformation. Turning one substance into another. Extracting something valuable from something ordinary. In computing, a similar transformation occurs, but in a different form.

Sand becomes silicon. Silicon becomes structure. Structure becomes computation. Computation becomes images, language, memory. The transformation is real, but abstract. Not material into material, but material into meaning. The comparison is metaphorical, but difficult to avoid. A process that takes something common and turns it into something that can hold human experience.

There is also a more grounded concern, one that does not require metaphor. That computational systems, especially those tied to large networks and algorithms, influence how people think. What is seen, what is repeated, what is reinforced.

At its most speculative edge, this becomes the idea that systems do not just process information, but shape perception. Not through intention, but through structure. By filtering, prioritizing, and repeating certain patterns, they can influence how reality is interpreted. This is not mystical, but it can feel that way. The system does not tell you what to think, but it changes what you are likely to encounter.

Another interpretation moves in the opposite direction. That machines are not separate from human thought, but extensions of it. That computation is a continuation of cognition, externalized into physical systems.

In this view, the boundary between human and machine becomes less clear. Not because machines become human, but because aspects of thinking, memory, and decision-making are offloaded into systems. The CPU does not think, but it performs operations that resemble parts of thinking. Over time, this creates a distributed form of cognition, where the process is no longer contained entirely within the individual.

This leads into a more philosophical question about determinism. A CPU operates through defined rules. Given the same input, it will produce the same output. It is entirely predictable in principle.

If more systems begin to operate in this way, or if reality itself can be described through similar rules, the question emerges whether everything is ultimately deterministic. Whether complexity gives the illusion of unpredictability, while underlying processes remain fixed. This is not unique to computing, but computing makes it visible.

Finally, there is the idea of layered abstraction as a model not just for systems, but for reality itself. Computing is built in layers. Physical behavior at the bottom, then electronics, then logic, then software, then interaction.

Each layer depends on the one beneath it, but does not need to fully understand it.

Some have drawn parallels between this and how reality might be structured. Physics giving rise to chemistry, chemistry to biology, biology to consciousness. Each layer emerging from the previous, but operating with its own rules and language.

In computing, this structure is deliberate. In reality, it is observed.

The comparison is not proof of anything.

But it is difficult to ignore.

These ideas do not change how systems work. The mechanisms remain the same. Electrons move, transistors switch, instructions execute.

But at the edges of understanding, where systems become too complex to follow intuitively, interpretation begins to take over.

Not as explanation.

But as a way to make sense of something that feels, at times, just slightly beyond it.

The image shows the underside of a DVD (Digital Versatile Disc), where the data is stored and read.

The reflective surface contains a single continuous spiral track that starts at the center and moves outward. Along this spiral are tiny microscopic marks called pits and lands, which encode digital information. A laser inside a DVD player reads these patterns by detecting differences in how light is reflected.

Although the surface appears smooth and shiny, it actually contains billions of tiny data points, allowing the disc to store large amounts of information such as video, audio, or software.

"DVD-Video bottom side" — by Ocrho, via Wikimedia Commons, Public Domain.

SONY
LTX400G
ULTRIUM 3
400/800GB

The image shows a Sony LTX400G data tape cartridge, a storage medium used for backing up and archiving large amounts of digital data. Inside the plastic casing is a long strip of magnetic tape that records information by storing it as magnetic patterns along its length. This type of cartridge belongs to the LTO (Linear Tape-Open) standard and was commonly used in servers and data centers. Although it appears simple, it can store large volumes of data and is designed for long-term reliability, making it useful for backups and archival storage rather than everyday access.

The image shows the inside of a 3.5-inch mechanical hard drive with its cover removed, revealing the physical components used to store data. At the center are one or more circular metal platters coated with magnetic material. These platters spin at high speed while a moving read/write head hovers just above the surface, recording and retrieving data by changing tiny magnetic patterns.

This method of storage is different from optical discs such as CDs and DVDs. Optical discs store data along a spiral track made of microscopic pits and lands on a reflective surface. A laser reads this information by detecting changes in reflected light, rather than using magnetism.

In contrast, the hard drive shown in the image relies on precise mechanical movement and magnetic storage, allowing for faster access and the ability to rewrite data many times. It represents a different approach to data storage, where spinning disks and moving parts work together to store large amounts of information efficiently.

"35-Desktop-Hard-Drive.jpg" — by Evan-Amos, via Wikimedia Commons, CC BY-SA 3.0.

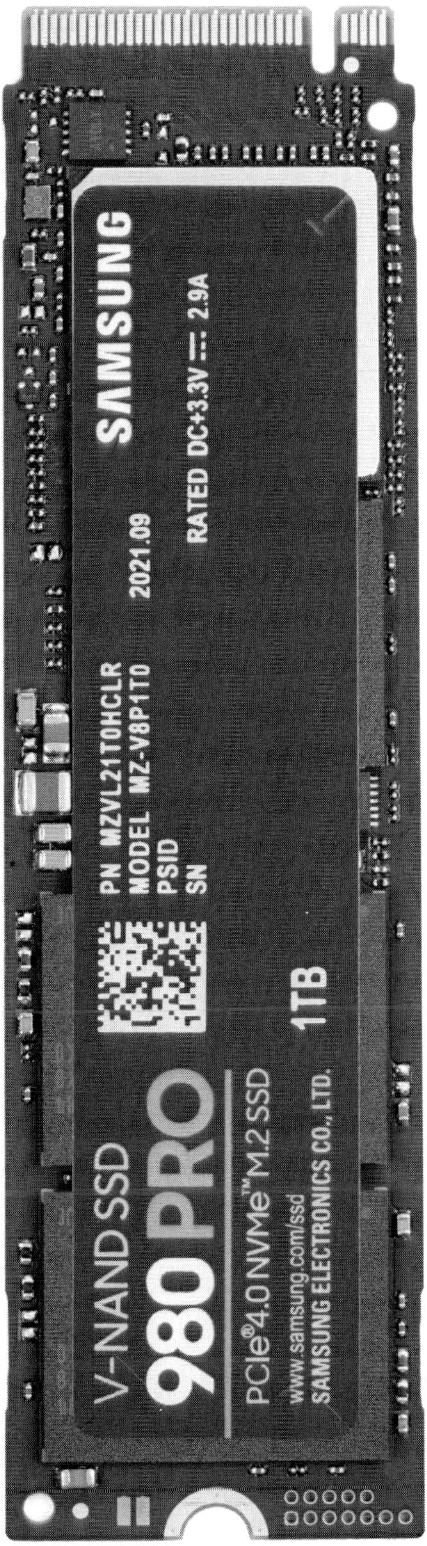
V-NAND SSD
980 PRO
PCIe®4.0 NVMe™ M.2 SSD
www.samsung.com/ssd
SAMSUNG ELECTRONICS CO., LTD.
1TB
PN MZVL21T0HCLR
MODEL MZ-V8P1T0
PSID
SN
2021.09
SAMSUNG
RATED DC+3.3V ⎓ 2.9A

The image shows a Samsung 980 PRO NVMe solid-state drive (SSD), a modern storage device used in computers to store data. It is a compact circuit board that plugs directly into a motherboard using the M.2 interface.

Unlike mechanical hard drives, this SSD has no moving parts. Instead, it stores data in flash memory chips, where information is kept as electrical charges inside tiny cells. A controller chip manages how data is written, read, and organized across the memory, ensuring speed and reliability.

The drive uses the NVMe protocol over PCIe, which allows it to communicate directly with the computer's processor at very high speeds. This makes it much faster than older storage technologies, enabling quick file access, fast system boot times, and high-performance data transfer.

Overall, the image represents a modern approach to data storage, where solid-state electronics replace mechanical components to achieve greater speed, durability, and efficiency.

A row of tall metal server racks filled with computer hardware belonging to the Internet Archive is shown in the image. It is installed inside the Bibliotheca Alexandrina in Egypt, forming part of a larger system designed for digital preservation.

Bibliotheca Alexandrina hosts a mirror of the Internet Archive through a partnership with the San Francisco–based nonprofit. In 2008, it received a major donation including 10 billion web pages (1996–2007), thousands of hours of TV broadcasts, archival films, and about 100 terabytes of data.

The archive was designed as a backup site to preserve digital heritage and became an important part of the Internet Archive's global redundancy system. It was later upgraded with Petabox technology, increasing storage capacity and supporting continued expansion of the digital archive in Egypt.

intel®
i486™ DX2™
A80486DX2-66
C3250272
SX645
INTEL ©1989

The image shows a CPU (central processing unit), often called the “brain” of a computer. It is a small electronic chip that performs calculations and executes instructions. Every action a computer takes, opening a webpage, sending a message, or loading a video is handled by the CPU.

A CPU works by following instructions step by step. It reads commands from memory, processes them using billions of tiny electronic switches called transistors, and produces results. Modern CPUs can perform billions of operations per second, allowing them to handle complex tasks almost instantly.

Without CPUs, the internet would not exist. The internet is not just cables and signals, it depends on devices constantly processing and routing data. Every server, router, and personal device uses CPUs to interpret data, decide where it should go, and respond to requests. Without this processing capability, data could not be understood, directed, or used in any meaningful way.

Also, without CPUs there would be no computing at all. No software could run, no data could be processed, and no digital systems could function. What makes CPUs remarkable is that they turn simple electrical signals into structured actions, enabling everything from basic calculations to global communication networks.

Chapter 17 – Final words

There is more that could be said, much more.

Entire volumes could be written about each part of what has been described here, every system, every shift, every layer of culture and influence. At the same time, far less could also be said. The Internet can be reduced to something simple, a network, a tool, a way of moving information from one place to another. Both perspectives are true, depending on how closely you choose to look.

This has been an attempt to stay somewhere in between.

Not to explain everything, but to make visible enough of it to understand what it has become.

Because once it was introduced at scale, something changed. The path forward was no longer only physical. Human development began to extend into something less tangible, shaped not just by environment and society, but by a constant flow of information that connects everything to everything else. The Internet did not replace the world, but it altered how the world is experienced and how it evolves.

The Internet carries laughter, knowledge, entertainment, distraction, learning, creation, connection. It also carries conflict, manipulation, misinformation, and things that are difficult to fully account for. It does not filter by intention. It reflects what moves through it, and what moves through it comes from people, systems, and everything in between.

Over time, it begins to resemble something larger than the sum of its parts.

Not a single entity, but a continuous activity. Always moving, always updating, always responding. Inputs become outputs, outputs become new inputs, and the process does not stop. It grows, adapts, and reshapes itself through use.

In that sense, it behaves less like a static system and more like a hive.

Not controlled from one place, not fully understood from any single perspective, but active, collective, and constantly in motion. Each participant contributes, whether intentionally or not, and the result is something that exists beyond any individual contribution.

And whatever it becomes next will not be decided in one place, or by one group, but through the same process that brought it here.

This book has been written with a balance in mind. It is meant to be accessible to someone encountering these ideas for the first time, while still offering depth to those already familiar with the subject. The Internet can be approached from many angles, technical, cultural, philosophical, and none of them exist in isolation. Understanding even a portion of it is enough to begin seeing how deeply it is embedded in everyday life.

With that understanding comes a more practical consideration. As connectivity has expanded, it has also moved closer to the individual. Devices that were once separate now exist within the same network. Phones, computers, televisions, appliances, all connected, often continuously. What appears as convenience is also exposure. A device connected to your home network is not isolated. It is part of a system that ultimately connects outward.

This does not mean that access is automatic or effortless, but it does mean that the possibility exists. If a device is poorly secured, wrongly configured, or left unprotected, it can become a point of entry. From there, other parts of the network may become visible. The distance between locations no longer matters in the same way. With sufficient knowledge and the right conditions, someone sitting in an internet café in Seoul could, in principle, reach into a poorly secured network in Paris, maybe someones home, not through physical presence, but through the same infrastructure that connects them both.

This is not a statement of constant risk, but a reminder of structure. The Internet connects by design. What is added to it becomes part of that connection. As more of everyday life becomes integrated into this network, awareness becomes part of participation. Not to withdraw from it, but to understand what it means to be connected.

And like everything else described here, it is part of the same system.

Always active. Always connected.

As The Internet can help and ruin. The Internet is neither good or bad, it is about how it is used.

Gain knowledge, build yourself.

Spread knowledge, spread love.

Made in United States
North Haven, CT
04 November 2026

21770485R00136